A HEART
WITHOUT
A HOME

A memoir about homelessness

through the eyes of a child

Nichole Anne Carpenter

A Heart Without A Home
By Nichole Anne Carpenter

Cover Design by Nichole Anne Carpenter

Copyright © 2016 by Nichole Anne Carpenter

I have tried to recreate events, locales and conversations from my memories of them. In order to maintain their anonymity in some instances I have changed the names of individuals and places, I may have changed some identifying characteristics and details such as physical properties, occupations and places of residence.

ISBN-13: 978-1530198344
ISBN-10: 1530198348

Intrabellus Inc.
PO Box
Orange, CA 92869

For information about special discounts available for bulk purchases, sales promotions, fund-raising, educational needs or to book Nichole to speak at your event, contact Intrabellus, Inc. Sales at 1-714-864-6394 or Sales@NicholeCarpenter.com.

Visit the author's website at **www.NicholeCarpenter.com**

A MESSAGE FROM THE AUTHOR

Thank you for taking the time to read my book. Over the years, many people have asked me to share my story and I am grateful for all of the love and support throughout this process.

My desire is for everyone that reads this to be blessed and to treat one another with more love and compassion. Please visit my website and let me know what you thought of the book.

If you would like to have me come speak at your event or to order copies of my book for your event please email me at, **Sales@NicholeCarpenter.com**.

Every week on my podcast, my guests reveal their personal struggles with homelessness. To hear their stories, and learn ways to make a positive difference in the world, visit **www.NicholeCarpenter.com**

THANKS

I want to thank so many people who helped me and supported me through the writing of this book.

First, I would like to thank you mother, Madge Carpenter, for her encouragement and advice. Mom you are my inspiration and my hero. I have watched you overcome so much and I am so grateful to have you in my life. I love you.

I would also like to thank my Aunt Kathryn Jolley. I never would have had my book ready in time without your help. Thank you and I love you.

Thank you to my church family at Spirit and Truth Worship Center. Your prayers and support throughout my life are what brought me to where I am today.

Thank you to all my friends and mentors at CEO Space International. Without your advice and support, I never would have attempted to write this book.

Thank you to all of my family. Your encouragement and support have been such a blessing in my life.

Most of all, I thank God for protecting me and guiding me. He promised that he has a plan and a purpose for my life (Jeremiah 29:11) and He has certainly proven that to be true.

CHAPTER 1

A trail of musty gray smoke rose in circling ribbons from a cigarette in the ashtray on the dresser. Across the rest of the dresser lay discarded sections of a newspaper, a couple of worn pieces of aluminum foil folded with tight creases into two small squares, a lighter, a pair of short straws, and a crumpled paper bag with an unopened pack of cigarettes. There was a small walkway between the dresser and the full-size mattress lying on the floor across the room. A variety of mismatched blankets and sheets covered the bed.

Among the folds of one of the blankets, a small form lay sleeping. Laying on her side, the girl, Nichole, curled her thin legs close to her stomach and then wrapped her arms around her teddy bear with its head tucked under her chin. Her light brown hair spread across the pillow and her face like a tangled spider web. She wore a royal blue nightgown that her grandmother had made her. Its sleeves and the bottom hem ruffled, and there was a thin row of lace on all of the edges. At the top of the collar was a tiny white rose. Since her grandma had passed away a few months before, Nichole had worn that same nightgown to bed every night.

Muffled shouts drifted in through the closed bedroom door, which led into the living room. The little girl began to stir awake at the noise. She stretched her arms above her head and then her feet straight out to her full length like a rigid marionette puppet of exactly four feet from head to toe. At nine years old, she was still small for her age. Her still-waking mind struggled to understand the noise that had woke her. As she lay still on the bed, she heard more shouting coming from the other room. Nichole rubbed the sleep from her eyes as she sat up on the bed.

A thick black blanket covered the window above her to block out any light from the sun during the day. Nichole turned to the window and crawled up onto her knees to find the small hole in the blanket from when a cigarette had gotten too close and burnt the fabric. The burn left a small hole with a jagged brown ring around it. Nichole reached up and peeked with one eye through the hole to see that it was still dark out. She turned to the clock next to the bed and read the time. It was 4:23 in the morning.

It was not strange for her mom to be up this early, but she was surprised to hear her dad's voice as well. Usually, her dad stayed in bed most of the day unless he had to go to work, which he had not done in a while. Her mother, Madge grew up on a farm in Idaho where they woke before the sun was up. Even after all of these years, she was still in the habit of waking up early as if she still had to go milk the cows before school.

They had only moved to California a few months ago after Madge's parents had died in a car crash. Nichole's father, Andy, had gotten out of jail around the same time, and he had suggested that they move from Utah, where Nichole had been born to Southern California where his family lived. Andy and Madge had struggled in Utah with drugs and alcohol. They figured starting over in a new place would do them both some good.

This was not a new idea for them. In fact, they had moved every few months over the years since before Nichole was born. From legal problems to money problems to bad relationships, they had stayed on the move for as long as Nichole could remember. From kindergarten to second grade, she had attended five different schools in different cities and sometimes even in different states. Now she was in the third grade, and she liked her new teacher and even had a best friend.

While Nichole was sitting on the bed hugging her teddy bear, her mom opened the door to the bedroom.

"Nichole, are you awake?" She whispered as her eyes tried to adjust to the darkness of the room.

"Yeah, is it time for school?"

"No Baby, you are not going to school today."

Nichole liked that her mom still called her "Baby" even though she was not really a baby. Madge had told her that no matter how big she got, she would always be her baby.

"Why?" Nichole asked, "Is today Saturday?"

"No, it is not Saturday. We have to move out today."

"We are moving again? Where are we going to go?"

"I do not know, Baby," her mom whispered and then her voice cracked from crying. Madge wiped a tear away from her green eyes. Nichole had always wished she had green eyes like her mom. Her eyes were more of a grayish blue, more like her dad.

"Is that why you and daddy were fighting?" Nichole crawled to the foot of the bed where her mom sat with her head in her hands. Sections of pitch black, wavy hair hung over Madge's face, except for the bit that she gathered back in a low barrette. Nichole wrapped her arms around her mom's neck and pulled her small frame up onto her mother's lap. Madge sat up straighter to make room to hold her daughter close.

"Yes, we will have to go because we have not paid the rent in a few months."

Nichole nodded. Money had always controlled their life. Nichole's father used to have a job as a taxi driver, but his boss had fired him. Andy had made up a story about one of his customers robbing him at knifepoint but in reality, he was just trying to keep more money for himself.

"Can't we just go to Granny and Grandpa's?" Nichole requested.

"Your dad said, 'no'. He already borrowed too much money from them. We will have to try to make it on our own." Madge sniffled and wiped the tears from her eyes.

Nichole had come to understand that family would help for so long, but, after a while, they just could not help anymore.

"Ok, Baby, you need to go get in the truck so we can go before the landlord wakes up."

"Do I need to get dressed first?"

Madge grabbed the paper bag off the dresser, took out the pack of cigarettes, and put them in her pocket.

"Just put your pants on and then put some extra clothes in this bag to take with us."

Nichole took the bag and slid off the bed. She opened her drawer on the bottom row of the dresser and pulled out her favorite pair of jeans. Sitting on the floor, she slid them on. She then gathered out three t-shirts, two pairs of socks and a few pairs of panties. She stuffed them all in the bag while her mom gathered up the foil, lighter, and straws on the dresser and put them in her other pocket. Madge picked up the burning cigarette in the ashtray, which was now a short stub and took a couple of puffs before squishing the tip in the tray. She exhaled a long slow trail of shabby white smoke.

Nichole stood to her feet and followed her mom out to the living room. Her father, Andy, was pacing back and forth in the room. He looked up when Madge and Nichole came out of the bedroom and began talking so fast Nichole could not understand everything he was saying. Aside from the steady stream of curse words, Nichole understood a few phrases, "Are you ready yet...He is going to come for the money...Got to go..."

Andy looked around the room wide-eyed as if to see if the answer to all of his problems might be lying on the floor somewhere. His mind hummed like an electric fan. After a dazed pause, he looked up at Madge and Nichole, who were standing in the middle of the room watching him.

"Ok, let's go." He clapped his hands and started to walk forward. As quick as he started forward, he turned on his heels and raced back through every single room of the small house, pulling out all of the drawers in the kitchen, opening and shutting all of the cupboards, and digging through piles of discarded papers on the floor. After a few minutes of running about like a startled deer on the road, he returned to the front room with only a handful of loose change to show for his last minute treasure hunt.

"Why are you still standing here? We have to go!" His words spilled out as if he had been standing there waiting on them instead of the other way around. He then walked passed them and went out the door.

Madge and Nichole looked at each other, and they followed him out the door. Nichole slipped her bare feet into her tennis shoes, which had been lying outside the front door. Without bothering to tie the laces, she followed her mom down the steep staircase. Her dad was standing there at the top with the key. He closed and locked the front door and then threw the key far into the trees behind the house and whispered, "Good luck finding that!" He finished his phrase with a verbal assault that he saved especially for their landlord and anybody else who needed money from him.

Madge tugged Nichole's arm and led her to their truck. Andy ran his fingers through his short blond hair that he always slicked straight back and chuckled at his own cleverness before following them down the stairs to the truck.

Their only vehicle was an old Datsun pickup truck. The paint had faded to a light blue with spots of rust showing through. There was a small cab space, with a bench seat and three seat belts. When all three of them were in the truck together, all of their knees touched in the tight space.

Nichole climbed in the middle seat so she could ride in between both of her parents. Since waking up and preparing to leave, she had never let go of her teddy bear, and she now hugged him tight against her lap. The cracked vinyl fabric of the seat pinched her leg, and she looked around for something to sit on. Stuffed behind the seat were a few worn blankets that her mom must have put in there earlier that morning. Nichole tugged one out and shimmied part of it under her. The rest she gathered around herself to block out the early morning chill.

Her parents each stood on either side of the truck with their doors wide open. Andy leaned inside across the seat and whispered to Madge on the other side, "We will have to get off the property before we can turn on the truck or else the landlord will wake up and catch us." Madge nodded, this was not the first time they had to leave somewhere in the middle of the night without being caught. Unfortunately, this was a familiar routine.

Andy sat in the driver's seat with one foot still hanging out the door and the other on the brake pedal. He turned the key just one click so that he could wiggle the gearshift to Neutral. He lifted his foot off the brake, and the small truck started to roll forward. Madge gripped her door with one hand and the door frame with the other and leaned forward to help push the truck. Andy hopped out of his seat with his left hand on the door and his right still on the steering wheel. He both pushed and forced the steering wheel to turn the truck down the driveway that circled around the landlord's house. The gravel road sounded off an echoing crunch as the tires rolled forward. Nichole clipped her seatbelt around herself, gathered her feet beside her, and tucked them under the blanket.

As her parents struggled and pushed, Nichole watched as they rolled past the horses in the stables that their landlord rented out to people in the city. Then they rolled past a row of orange trees where she used to climb and catch tree frogs. Finally, they rolled past the tiny creek that she had played in. Just before they reached the road, the gravel driveway curved upward. As they approached the incline, Andy and Madge dug their feet in harder and pushed faster to gain enough momentum to heave the truck up and over. At last, they pushed the truck off the gravel and onto the paved road. Both of her parents jumped in the truck.

Andy turned the keys in the ignition, and it roared to life. He shifted into Drive and pressed down on the gas pedal. He slowed briefly as they approached a stop sign. When he saw no other cars within eyesight, he accelerated and whipped a left turn. As they sped around the turn, Madge's passenger side door swung open. The door latch had broken many months before, but Andy had never bothered to fix it. Madge clung to the back of the seat with one hand and to the dashboard with the other. She held on until they were driving straight forward again and then reached out and slammed the door shut.

"Andy, you need to fix this door!" Madge screamed at him.

"Huh?" He looked at her with an expression as blank as a stark white page. His mind was so preoccupied; he had not even noticed that one of his passengers had nearly fallen out of the truck.

"Whatever!" Madge exclaimed, pulled her seatbelt across her, and buckled it before she ended up sprawled out on the road like a piece of roadkill.

They drove passed his parents' house and his sister's house. If only Andy had not already burned their bridges, then they could just go and stay with family again, like Madge and Nichole did in Utah whenever Andy had gone to jail. At least, they were all together. Some family is better than no family.

"Where are we going to go, Daddy?" Nichole asked.

"How should I know?" he replied. "I can't think right now. I need a fix."

"Come here, Baby, get some rest." Madge tugged Nichole's shoulder towards her so that she could lay her head down on her lap. Nichole loosened the seatbelt across her lap so that she could turn on her side. She then arranged the blanket so that she could lie down while still clutching her teddy bear. Nichole stretched out her legs until her feet rested on her father's lap. She then reached down and tugged the blanket over her shoes. Madge stroked her straight brown hair until Nichole's eyes started to droop and she fell to sleep.

CHAPTER 2

Andy stared at the narrow road stretching ahead of him. His mind swam with mixed thoughts as he drove into the blurred distance waiting for daylight. They had nowhere to go and no plan.

Nichole stirred as she lay sleeping next to him with her feet resting on his lap. A rush of overwhelming emotion flooded Andy's veins. He shuddered and his mouth got dry as if it was full of cotton balls. His head began to throb like a heavy drum. He was already in the habit of having to look out for himself, but now he had his daughter and wife to take care of too.

The sun began to climb over the horizon in his rear view mirror, spraying the sky with flecks of gold on the edges of the clouds. Andy turned off the road and into a gas station. Behind the dusty glass on the dashboard, he could see the gas meter resting closely against empty. He pulled forward next to the first gas pump and turned off the truck. He slid Nichole's feet off his lap as he opened his door and stepped out.

The sudden movement woke Nichole, and she squinted as she opened her eyes to the bright morning light.

"Where are we?" Nichole asked her mom as she stretched her arms up to lift herself into a seated position.

"We are at a gas station." Madge helped Nichole out from the blanket.

"I am hungry," Nichole whispered as she rubbed her eyes.

Leaning his head back in the truck, Andy called out to Nichole, "Check for change." He gestured to the truck seat as he stood leaning against the open door frame.

Nichole unbuckled her seatbelt like a racehorse released from the gate. Searching for loose change was one of her favorite activities. If she found enough, she could use some of it to buy a snack and then the rest would go toward their gas. Plus she loved to count. Math had been her favorite subject whenever she got to go to school.

While Nichole searched, Madge opened her door and stepped out. She pulled the pack of cigarettes and lighter from her pocket.

"I am going for a smoke," she mumbled to Andy and Nichole, and she walked away from the truck.

"Okay!" Nichole answered without looking up as she dug her fingers in the crevices of the seat to reveal pennies, nickels, and dimes. If she found any quarters, she set them in a neat pile on the driver's seat for her dad.

Madge walked away from the truck to a grassy area, where she sat on the curb and lit her cigarette. She was so mad that Andy had let things get this bad, and she felt helpless to do anything about it. Whenever it had been just her and Nichole, they always had a place to live. Sure, they often had to stay with one of her sisters or her parents, but they never had to leave places in the middle of the night, except when Andy was around. Now Madge was hundreds of miles away from any of her family and she could never go back to her parents since they had just passed away. Madge would have given anything to hug her mother just once more.

"Here you go, Daddy!" Nichole called out and handed Andy five grimy quarters. He took the quarters and walked over to where Madge was savoring her cigarette. She handed what remained of it to him to finish, got up, and walked back to the truck. When she returned to the truck, Nichole was counting the rest of the change she had found.

"Mommy, I have $2.63! Can I get some food?" Nichole looked up when Madge slid into the seat next to her.

"Sure, Baby. Let's go." Madge climbed back out of the truck and took Nichole's hand. Together they walked into the gas station convenience store. Nichole examined the display of potato chips and finally selected a bright orange bag of Cheetos.

Outside, Andy used one of the quarters to buy a newspaper from the coin-operated rack. He tucked the paper under his arm and walked over to the pay phone behind the store. Using the second quarter, he dropped it in the slot and pulled a piece of torn paper from his pocket that had a phone number scribbled across it. He pressed each number on the keypad pausing between each to make sure that he got every single number right. He pulled the phone up to his ear and held it there with his shoulder. He turned his back to the pay phone and leaned against the side of it while looking around him to make sure nobody was listening to him. After five rings a man answered on the other end of the phone, "Who is this?"

"This is Andy! Is Hector there?"

"I am Hector. How did you get my number?"

"Mario gave me your number! I need to make a purchase." Andy looked around again make sure nobody was within earshot.

Hector rattled off an address for Andy to meet him at in twenty minutes. Hanging up the phone, Andy checked his pockets to count how much change he had left from what Nichole had found and from what he had gathered from the house before they left. Eight dollars and sixty-six cents in coins plus the only twenty-dollar bill he had left from his last paycheck.

Andy walked into the convenience store as Madge and Nichole were walking out with their bag of Cheetos. He put the pile of change on the counter and informed the cashier which gas pump he would be using. He then briskly walked out the door and rushed to dispense the seven gallons of gas that the change afforded him.

Once he finished dispensing the gas, he climbed in the truck. Madge and Nichole had already buckled their seatbelts and Nichole was munching on her breakfast of crunchy cheesy chips and licking the bright orange powder off her fingertips.

"I found a dealer," Andy whispered to Madge. "It's the guy that Mario told me about."

"Can we go now?" Madge asked anxiously.

"Yes. He is waiting for us."

Andy shifted the truck into gear and turned onto the main road with a focused determination. To get their drug fix.

Andy and Madge were not born in drug-filled homes like their daughter was. They both had Christian parents and siblings who were successful. Andy had struggled to find approval growing up since he was a hyperactive child, and he had always pushed the boundaries and resisted rules. He had an unquenchable curiosity and his parents tried their best to discipline him in hopes of guiding him on a profitable path. Unfortunately, the discipline did not set him on a straight path but rather fueled in him a self- righteous rage and self-pity that he gradually learned to numb with drugs.

Madge had grown up in a dull small town in the country and had looked for any opportunity to get away and find excitement. She found her excitement in parties filled with alcohol and drug use.

Andy and Madge had met in a bar where a mutual friend worked and built their relationship on their shared interests in drugs and general recklessness.

Gradually, years of wild living had dragged them to their current situation, where they had both succumbed to heroin addiction. Not with needles, though! Andy hated needles. Plus, he did not want to risk dying from some worthless disease by a tainted needle. Instead, they would buy heroin in its black tar form. This way, they could smoke it. Even without being shooters, the addiction still consumed their lives.

Andy maneuvered the roads with practiced ease. He knew the area well since this was where he had grown up. Finally, they pulled into a narrow alley. On each side lay overturned trashcans with garbage spilling into the middle of the road. Several stray cats scampered out of the way, as Andy coasted the truck to a stop.

"Stay here" he instructed his passengers as he got out and walked up to a group of men standing in an open garage. He spoke with them for a moment before one of them pointed to the gate around the corner. Andy slipped behind the garage and returned less than a minute later with his hands in his pockets.

He jumped in the truck and sped off. "What a jerk! He is a criminal!" Andy fumed, "He only gave me three-quarters of what he promised."

An explosive string of profanity erupted out of his mouth as he pounded his fists on the steering wheel and dashboard.

Nichole stroked her teddy bear's head and hummed a song softly so that only she could hear it. After driving around for twenty minutes, Andy finally pulled into an empty lot of a city park. He faced the car toward the playground.

"Can I go play?" Nichole perked up at the sight of the playground. Andy nodded, but Madge cautioned, "Just stay where we can see you."

Nichole crawled across her mom's lap, opened the door and jumped out. The fresh air had a slight chill to it, and Nichole turned back to the truck. She was still wearing her nightgown from the night before, and it did not provide much protection against the cold. She reached into her bag of clothes lying at her mother's feet and pulled out her pink sweatshirt. She slipped her arms in the sleeves and zipped the front over her nightgown. She then turned again and headed to the playground. Madge pulled the door closed as Nichole ran to the swings.

Andy reached into his pocket and pulled out a tiny black ball of heroin wrapped in Saran Wrap and enclosed in a tiny zip-lock bag. Madge pulled out the squares of foil, the lighter, and the cut straws from her pocket. She handed Andy one straw and foil square and they each took turns using the lighter.

Andy opened the zip-lock bag carefully. He peeled away the Saran wrap to reveal the shiny black ball of heroin. With his fingernails, he tugged off a small piece and rolled it between his fingers before passing it to Madge. While she arranged the ball onto her piece of foil, he pulled off a bigger ball for himself. He then pressed it in the center of the foil. With his free hand, he grabbed the straw and placed it between his lips. Finally, he held the foil flat with his fingers and held the lit lighter beneath it. After a moment, the heroin started to bubble and burn. A thin trail of dark smoke rose from the foil. Using his straw, he sucked in the smoke making sure not to miss any. After a long and deep inhale, Andy passed the lighter to Madge. He held his breath for as long as he could and allowed the smoke to fill his lungs, absorbing it into his blood and enveloping his tortured mind.

Madge repeated the same routine though her hit was not nearly as strong since she took a much smaller amount. Immediately the stress and anxiety faded, and a sense of euphoria enveloped them. In the high, they had no problems, no worries, nothing to fear. Andy's eyes drooped closed and fluttered. His head rocked forward and back like a fishing popper in the lake.

After about five minutes, Madge had recomposed herself and stepped out of the truck to go watch Nichole.

"Mommy! Watch me!" Nichole screamed.

Madge stopped at watch her daughter. Nichole stood behind a swing with her hands gripping the sides. She stepped each foot backward dragging them across the sand until the swing was taut and she extended her arms in front of her. She then lunged forward running under the swing, still holding onto the chains with both hands. The swing reached its limit and flung Nichole's body out underneath it. Her feet flew out from under her and flipped over her head until she landed with her stomach on the swing and was soaring back and forth. "Tada!" Nichole stretched out both hands to her sides and she swung on her stomach like a superhero flying through the air.

Madge's heart jumped in her chest at her daughter's stunt. She could not catch her breath until she saw her daughter land in one piece on the swing.

"Where did you learn that?"

"I do it every single day at school," Nichole answered.

"You almost gave me a heart attack!" Madge held her hand against her chest.

Nichole giggled and dragged her feet in the sand below the swing to bring it to a stop. She then ran to her mom and wrapped her arms around her waist. "I love you, Mommy! I am sorry I scared you. I won't get hurt."

"I love you more." Madge wrapped her arms around her daughter.

When Madge released her, Nichole ran back to the swing and repeated her stunt while her mom sat on the grass watching.

After about an hour, Andy finally got out of the truck and walked to where Madge was sitting on the grass.

"What are we going to do now?" she asked him.

"I do not know. We cannot go to my family again. And Mario does not have a place to stay right now either." He lay down on the grass and stared up in the sky above.

"We have to sleep somewhere." Madge urged him.

"I already know that! Give me a break!" Andy cursed and lifted his arm across his eyes to shield them from the sun.

"How much money do we have left?" She continued.

"We only have ten dollars."

"We cannot live off ten dollars!"

"You think I don't know that?" Andy stood up, threw his arms in the air, and walked back to the truck.

After another twenty minutes, Nichole ran back to where Madge waited. Nichole plopped down in her lap. "Can I go to school tomorrow, Mommy?"

"Maybe. We will see." Madge stroked Nichole's hair away from her face.

"I like school. My teacher is nice, I have a best friend, and I got one hundred percent on my math worksheet. My teacher put a sticker on it and hung it on the wall. If I go to school tomorrow, I will bring it home so I can show you." Nichole rambled along.

Madge stared off into the distance, "We don't have a home right now, baby."

"Well, I mean I can bring it to you and Daddy. You are my home."

Madge hugged Nichole close and allowed her own tears to flow down her cheeks.

Nichole placed both her hands on Madge's cheeks and rubbed the tears away. "It's ok, Mommy. When I grow up, I will take care of you. You will not have to feel scared or sad ever again."

After sitting for a few more minutes, Madge noticed that the sun had started to drop in the sky, and the shadows around them were stretching across the field.

"Let's go back to the truck." Madge held Nichole's hand, and, after Nichole stood to her feet, she tugged her mom's arm to pull her up to her feet. They walked hand in hand back to the truck.

Madge opened the door and Nichole climbed up onto the seat next to her dad, who was reading the newspaper that he had purchased that morning. He had finished several sections of the paper and had strewn them across the floorboard of the passenger seat. Madge got in and stepped on top of the pile of papers, crumbling them under her shoes.

"Are there any comics in there, Daddy?" Nichole leaned against Andy's shoulder and looked at the paper he was reading.

He turned and looked at her eager, trusting face. "Sure. Anything for my girl," he flipped through the sections and pulled out the page that had the comics and word puzzles. "Here you go." He passed it to Nichole.

"Mommy, will you read to me?" Nichole lifted the paper in front of Madge's face.

"Sure, Baby."

CHAPTER 3

As the sun began to set, the street lights flickered on in the parking lot where they sat in the truck. They hadn't realized how much time had passed.

"Daddy, where are we going to sleep tonight?" Nichole looked up at him with the unconditional trust only a child can offer.

"I think we are going to sleep here in the truck tonight," He mumbled.

"Like camping?"

"Yes," Andy agreed, "We are camping tonight."

"Cool!" Nichole grinned.

From somewhere behind them there was a bright flash, and then they heard a loud cracking boom.

"AAHH! WHAT WAS THAT?" Nichole scampered onto her mom's lap and tied her arms around her neck.

Andy peered in the rearview mirror as the second explosion erupted and grinned. "Don't worry. It's something good. I will show you."

He started up the truck and backed it up just enough to turn around and face the other direction. As he turned the truck around, there continued to be the same series of light and sound explosions. Once they were facing the other direction they were able to see looming over their heads a beautiful explosion of colors.

"Fireworks!" Nichole cried out.

"They must be from Disneyland," Andy explained, "We are less than a mile away."

Nichole slid off of her mother's lap and back onto the seat between her parents. She reached behind the seat to pull her blanket back out. She gathered it around herself and stretched out the sides so that her parents could enjoy the warmth of the blanket also. With a contented sigh, she gazed up at the night sky, watching the colors and shapes bursting overhead.

Small spots of light would fly up overhead and disappear for less than a second before bursting in a ball of hundreds of dots of light. When they burst, it looked like the ball was going to grow until it dropped right on top of them. One after another, different colored balls and rings flashed overhead.

"It looks like they are going to land on us," Nichole marveled.

"It's ok, Baby, we are safe," Madge reassured her and wrapped her arm around Nichole's shoulders.

"I know, Mommy. You will take care of me," came her soft reply.

Madge and Andy glanced at one another over Nichole's head. Nichole trusted them completely, but they were not so sure they could live up to it.

After a few minutes, Andy grew tired of watching the fireworks and picked his newspaper back up. On the page in front of him was an article about the growth in the rates for paper recycling. The article read, "...a ton of newspaper--enough to fill a pickup truck--will fetch between $100 and $150 at local collection centers." Andy paused and wished that he had access to truckloads worth of newspaper, but the answer came to him further down in the article when he got to the part that said, "...newspaper collectors with pickup trucks--called scavengers by cities and resourceful entrepreneurs by recycling centers--snatch newspapers from municipal recycling bins and cash them in." (LA Times; Read It and Reap: Newspaper Recycling Is Big Business These Days; July 08, 1995; Rebecca Mowbry)

"I know how we can get some money!" Andy shouted.

Nichole was too enthralled with the fireworks to hear him. Madge leaned her head over Nichole's to see what he was pointing to.

"Tomorrow we are going newspaper hunting," Andy explained.

"You have got to be kidding me!" Madge whispered.

"We can make some good money, and then we can get a place to stay," Andy tried to convince her.

"It says right there in the article that it is illegal." Madge jabbed her finger at the words on the page.

"It will work." Andy insisted.

Finally, the fireworks ended and Nichole settled back in the seat. "I am sleepy," She yawned. She then leaned over and picked up her teddy bear off the floor. Nichole tucked it under her chin and snuggled back under the blanket. She rested her head on her mom's shoulder and her eyes fluttered closed.

Andy continued trying to convince Madge that the newspaper recycling was their best option at this point, and after his desperate pleading she finally consented so that he would let her go to sleep.

CHAPTER 4

At the first glimpse of sunlight, Andy's eyes fluttered open. He rolled his head forward trying to loosen the knots that had formed in his neck and shoulders from sleeping in a seated position all night.

In the seat next to him, Nichole was still asleep. She had laid down during the night and stretched out with her feet across his lap and her head on Madge's lap.

"Are you awake?" Andy whispered to Madge.

Madge tilted her head toward him and nodded, "Yes. I only slept for about an hour."

"Well, I am going to get us some money today, so you do not have to worry about anything," he reminded her about their conversation the night before.

Madge rolled her eyes. She knew she could not believe his promises anymore.

Andy started the truck and eased his foot off the brake so that they could coast out of the parking lot. Nichole shifted but did not wake up.

"I need to find where people leave out their recycling bins," Andy thought out loud.

"There is probably a collection schedule." Madge pointed out.

After driving around for a half hour, he found a street where each house had a brown and blue trash bin set out on the curb. The blue bins were for recycling and the brown were for trash. Andy stopped at each recycle bin and dumped its entire contents in the bed of his truck. After two hours of collecting, he had gathered a small pile in the corner of the truck bed. Finally, he climbed back in the truck, sweating and exhausted.

"Let's go see how much we can get for this," he announced, confident that his labor was not in vain.

When they arrived at the recycling center, a line of cars and trucks had already formed at the large scales. One of the workers looked in the truck and signaled for Andy to pull over in the parking lot. The worker brought over a trash bin on wheels and indicated for Andy to put the paper products in one and cans in another. After dumping everything into the round bins, the worker wheeled them over to his small scale, punched a few buttons and wrote a note on a receipt. "Take this to the window," he said, pointing to the green building nearby. Andy joined the line in front of the cashier window, and, when it was his turn, he handed over the receipt and the cashier handed him back $17.93. "That's it?" he stammered.

"That's it. Next!" The cashier called out.

Andy walked back to the truck where Madge was helping Nichole who had just woken up, change out of the pajamas that she had worn the entire day before and into a clean outfit while hiding under the blanket.

"How did you do?" Madge asked when Andy jumped in the truck.

"Not even twenty dollars," He fumed. "There has to be another way!" Jumping back out of the truck he called out, "I will be right back!"

Striding over to one of the cars in line for the large scale, Andy dipped his head to look in through the passenger window. He talked with the driver for a minute and then jogged back to the truck. "I got it! Let's go!" He shifted the truck in gear, and they sped away.

"What are you going to do?" Madge looked at him sideways. She had been cultivating a growing suspicion of the things that got Andy excited over the years. They too often resulted in danger or jail time.

"We need to hit the big dumpsters and where there are a lot of them," he explained. "Like condos, apartments, and office complexes."

Over the next several hours, they drove from community to community, where Andy would drive from one dumpster to the next, digging through them and pulling out stacks of news and other papers.

Madge and Nichole sat in the car waiting while he worked. The thought of getting smelly and dirty and then someone seeing them digging through the trash was far too embarrassing for both of them. As they sat in the truck while Andy dug through the trash, a woman and young girl walked by on the other side of the parking lot. Nichole slid down onto the floorboard of the seat and ducked her head down low. She held her teddy bear and sweatshirt over her head so that they could not see her sitting in the truck as Andy tossed garbage in the back.

Madge tried to get her to sit back up on the seat beside her but Nichole would not budge. "But, Mommy, what if that girl is from my school, and they see me? Can I just go to school tomorrow instead of this?"

"I will ask your dad." Madge answered and rested her hand on top of Nichole's head until the woman and girl had walked past. "They are gone now." Madge tugged on her arm. "There is no one around to see us."

Nichole lifted herself off of the cramped floor one inch at a time until she ended up back on her seat. She looked all around the truck before sitting back calmly.

By the end of the day, the bed of the truck was nearly overflowing with paper. Andy drove to the recycling center. As they sped down the road, pieces of newspaper got caught in the wind and flew out of the truck.

At last, they pulled up to the large scale at the recycling center. The scale worker noted the weight of the full truck and signaled for Andy to go ahead and dump out the paper in the enormous mounds that they had. After emptying all of the paper out of the truck, Andy pulled back to the scale to get the weight of the empty truck.

The worker calculated the weight difference onto a receipt and handed it to Andy instructing them to go to the cashier to collect their money. This time, Andy got $78.

He ran back to the truck exclaiming, "I told you it would work!" He threw the pile of cash in Madge's lap. "Not bad for dumpster diving, is it?!" Madge looked down at the bills spilled across her lap. Struggling to believe that they got all of that money just from gathering papers out of the trash, she looked back up at Andy. "We can do this!"

Her mom's excitement was infectious and Nichole joined in the excitement along with her parents. She knew their first priority was to get drugs because if her parents went into withdrawals they would all be in trouble. "Mommy, Daddy, after you get well, can we go get some food?"

Andy grinned, "Of course! Where do you want to eat?"

Nichole tapped her finger on her cheek as she pondered. "Can we have McDonald's?"

"That sounds good to me!" Andy answered.

Pulling out of the recycling center, he headed straight from the nearest McDonald's. "I want a cheeseburger with no lettuce, and no tomatoes, and no mustard," Nichole shouted into the intercom at the drive-thru.

Andy chuckled, "You are just like your dad, aren't you?" He turned and added to their order, "Make that two cheeseburgers with ketchup only".

"You two do not know how to enjoy a good burger," Madge shook her head as she ordered her burger with all of the toppings.

The family shared an order of fries and a chocolate milkshake. Madge peeled the lid off of the milkshake and they all took turns dipping their fries in it and scooping out a clump of the chocolate ice cream on top of the fry. Nichole developed a chocolate ring around her mouth as she savored the sweet and salty blend.

As they ate, Andy drove to a nearby pay phone to arrange to buy some heroin while they had some extra cash.

They drove to a park, and, as they parked near the curb on the street, Andy noticed a group of teen boys hanging out around one of the picnic tables. He could tell by the colors they were wearing that they belonged to a local gang. While they sat in the truck and waited for Andy's dealer to arrive, Andy instructed Nichole how to behave. "Never look someone in the eye," he warned her. "They may think that you are challenging them or disrespecting them."

Nichole nodded with fear and absolute trust in her father as he explained to her what gangsters might do to a young girl like her if she was not careful.

Finally, his dealer arrived, and Andy got the money ready in his hand as the dealer approached their truck. He stopped at Andy's door and reached his hand inside while glancing around them to make sure the coast was clear. Andy handed him the roll of cash. The dealer then dropped a small plastic baggie in Andy's lap and walked away.

After the exchange, they drove to a secluded parking lot, where Andy and Madge took their heroin fix. While she waited in the back of the truck for them to finish, Nichole ate her burger, fries, and milkshake while humming a tune softly to herself.

As night began to approach, without any further discussion, the family tucked their blankets around them just as they had done the night before.

Over the next several days, they settled into a familiar routine of dumpster diving, recycling, eating, getting their drug fix, and sleeping.

Some mornings someone would catch them sleeping in the truck and would ask them to leave. Usually, Nichole managed to sleep right through the whole ordeal, covered by the piles of blankets stretched across her parents' laps.

After a while, Nichole stopped worrying about other kids seeing her in the dumpsters. She figured the kids at school did not even remember her anymore. Nichole started joining her parents and sometimes she would even find discarded toys and clothes that fit her. She would retrieve discarded toothbrushes and use them to sweep the dirt away from the ledges of the dumpster and would pretend like she was Cinderella in an urban forest.

One day while digging through a dumpster, while Andy and Madge were searching for blankets and newspapers, Nichole found a used pair of kid's roller blades.

While her parents continued digging for more newspapers, Nichole sat on the dirty concrete and tried them on. They fit perfectly! "Mommy, Mommy! Look what I found!" Nichole attempted to stand up and rolled forward, falling right in her mother's arms.

"Well, look at you!" Madge held onto Nichole's arm so that she could stand up straight. "Do you know how to use those?"

Nichole legs wobbled as her ankles stretched from side to side without the strength to hold them straight on the narrow rows of wheels. She attempted to let go of her mother's arms and teetered before grasping back on. "I can learn!" Nichole smiled with her eyes squinting and gave a confident nod. She released one finger at a time from her grasp on her mom's arm. Nichole bent down in a swatted position; she used her hands to push off of the ground and rolled straight ahead. Madge laughed at her daughter's creativity.

Once they finished collecting from that dumpster, Nichole wheeled herself, as she continued to squat over the rollerblades as though it was a miniature wheelchair. She got back to the truck, and Madge helped hoist her in, rollerblades and all.

Every day Nichole continued to practice and got better and better on the rollerblades. After a while, she was racing from one dumpster to the next as Andy drove the truck around. Sometimes she would even be sneaky and grab ahold of the back of the truck as Andy drove down the alleys. She would lock her ankles straight and bend her knees slightly while holding onto the tailgate of the truck. Andy would drive extra slow to make sure that she never got hurt.

Nichole taught herself how to turn her feet so that she could spin in circles and even managed to ride over speed bumps without falling down.

After asking nearly every day for weeks, Nichole had finally stopped asking her dad if she could go back to school. She knew his answer would always be the same: "We will take you to get enrolled tomorrow." Nichole knew that "tomorrow" would never be today.

In one neighborhood of condos, one young man noticed the family's efforts. He decided to place his newspapers on the ground beside the dumpster so they would not have to dig for it. Whenever he was home when they came by, he would even give Nichole her own dollar. One day when they stopped by he had a bucket of beads that snapped together. He explained that he saw them in a store and bought them just for her.

After a few months, the family did not even notice the saturated smells in the dumpsters. The smell was still a ripe blend of decaying foods, soiled diapers, used band aids, and damp papers but it had become a part of their routine and almost represented a sense of security for them. They would swipe wriggling maggots aside while looking for papers. They would shake out worn clothes that people had thrown away and rinse them under a hose in the park before wearing them. They did not even notice that they had begun to smell too since they did not have a better way to wash.

While at the recycling center one afternoon, Andy met an older gentleman who was turning in his collection of recyclables from his business. The man invited Andy to bring his family by his store sometime and then he would see if there was a way he could help them. It turned out that the man owned a small donut shop near where the family used to live.

That evening as Andy drove around to find a new place to park for the night, he told Madge and Nichole about the man. Madge struggled to trust people and automatically wondered, "What does he want from us?"

"I do not know," Andy shrugged his shoulders. "He said he may be able to help us out a little."

Andy pulled to the side of the road under a large tree. The street was all dark and the nearest house was half a block away. "This should do for tonight." He shifted the truck into park and turned off the engine.

"We need to sleep in a real bed one of these nights, Andy!" Madge began on her usual list of things that they needed to do. "We also need to shower and get some clean clothes. And Nichole needs to go back to school!"

"Okay, we will tomorrow." Andy waved her off with the same tired answer that he gave for everything that he could not provide. The fact was, if they were to enroll Nichole in school, then the teachers would most likely suspect something, and she could get taken away from them.

Andy groaned and climbed out of the truck to take a short walk and smoke a cigarette. In the darkness, you could not see anything except for the burning tip of the cigarette.

Madge and Nichole worked together to pull out their blankets from behind the seat. They arranged them with a layer underneath them and several across their lap. They had grown accustomed to making their seat into a small bed each night. There still was not enough room for them to all fit comfortably, but they used the blankets propped up against the doors and windows it provided some cushion and warmth as Andy and Madge slept sitting up.

"I do wish I could go to school," Nichole whispered to her mom.

"I know, Baby."

"You know what else I wish?" Nichole looked up at her mom.

"What is that?" She asked.

"I wish I could have a bubble bath and watch cartoons."

"Maybe someday, Baby," Madge stroked her hair and choked on a sob. She beat herself up over the fact that she could not provide for her daughter's simple desires.

Nichole laid her head down on her mom's lap to get ready for sleep. She reached her hand out from under the blanket and gripped her mom's hand. "Remember what Daddy said? Tomorrow maybe we will get to have donuts!"

"That is right, he did say that! Maybe we will." Madge smiled down at Nichole. She was so proud that her daughter continued to see the brighter side of things no matter what they were going through.

As Nichole drifted to sleep, Andy finally returned to the truck. He lifted her legs off of his seat, slid in, and set her feet across his lap. He tugged a corner of the blankets loose to tuck them around her bare feet. While Nichole slept, her parents smoked the last hit of heroin for the night.

CHAPTER 5

Early the next morning, Nichole was the first to wake up. Nichole was so excited to go visit the donut shop that she shook her father awake. Once she woke him up, Andy started up the truck and they headed for Looney's Donuts. In his grogginess, Andy did not even notice that the gas tank meter had been leaning on empty for quite a while.

Driving along the freeway, the truck began to sputter and jolt as the gas tank ran empty. "Help me rock the truck!" Andy called to his wife and daughter. "There might be enough gas in there to get us to the next gas station." Andy gripped his left hand on the window frame and rocked his body from side to side. Madge and Nichole joined him and it stirred the little remaining gas in the tank to find its way to the fuel line.

As they approached the next exit, the truck ran completely dry and started to slow to a stop. Andy cursed and turned the truck toward the exit. Using the slope of the off ramp, they coasted off the freeway before rolling to a stop at the bottom of the ramp. Andy checked over his shoulder to see if any cars were behind them. At least, the coast was clear.

"We will have to push," he shouted to Madge.

Madge opened her door, stepped out of her seat, and gripped the door frame. Together they got the truck rolling forward. "We may be able to coast it into the gas station on the corner," Andy shouted across the truck. Leaning into the weight of the truck, they pushed with all of their might. Finally, the truck gained enough momentum to roll on its own and Andy jumped into the driver's seat keeping the door ajar and one leg still dangling out in case he needed to jump back out again.

Madge jumped back into the truck. She almost lost her footing for a moment as it rolled faster. The truck rolled across the intersection as the light was changing from yellow to red. Approaching the gas station entrance, Andy and Madge had to jump back out to push the truck up the curb. A young man was walking by, and, seeing their predicament, he ran behind the truck and helped push it into the gas station.

"Thank you," Andy called out and nodded.

"No problem," the man waved and continued on his walk.

At the gas pump, Andy set Nichole to her task of checking the cracks around the seat for fallen change. Nichole recovered two dollars and nineteen cents. Handing the change to her dad, she asked, "Can I pretend to drive while you are getting the gas, Daddy?"

"Sure. Just don't move the gear shift; okay?!"

"Yes, Daddy," she answered.

Andy took the change and walked to the cashier to pay. Nichole slid onto the driver's seat and wrapped her fingers around the steering wheel. "Vroom," she called out as she slid her hands around and around the wheel, pretending to race in circles. Instead of touching the gearshift, she decided to use the levers around the steering wheel.

Click! The lever moved up and she pretended to go faster. Click! The lever went down and she pretended to be screeching to a stop. Her feet could not reach the pedals, so she just tucked them under herself so she could see over the steering wheel.

When he finished pumping the gas, Andy opened the door and signaled for Nichole to scoot over. She slid to the middle and immediately put her seat belt back on. Andy turned the ignition and the truck turned on, but so did the blinkers and windshield wipers. Madge laughed aloud at Andy's surprise. "Who did this?" Andy pretended to be stern. Nichole giggled and ducked her head down before looking back up at her dad, and they all started laughing together.

Finally, Andy pulled out of the gas station and headed for the donut shop. They drove up in the hills where they used to live, and Nichole gazed out the window at their old street as they drove by. A few minutes later, they pulled into a shopping center parking lot and there in the corner was Looney's Donuts. Nichole clapped and cried out, "There is the donut shop!"

When they walked in the front door, there was already a crowd of people in line selecting their morning donuts. The man behind the counter waved to Andy and indicated for them to stick around until the crowd died down. While they were waiting, Nichole pressed her way through the crowd to the glass cabinet. From top to bottom, she gazed at every single sort of donut you could ever wish for. There are regular donuts with shimmering glaze, ones with chocolate frosting across the top, apple fritters, bear claws, long ones with different colored frosting, donuts with rainbow sprinkles, donut holes, donuts with cream filling and fruit filling, and there on the top shelf right in the middle was Nichole's favorite, a chocolate donut with chocolate frosting and chocolate sprinkles.

The smells filled the air. The sweet, sugary scents wafted through her nose and made her tummy rumble. Anxious to get her donut, Nichole looked around the shop for her parents. The noise of all of the customers placing orders, talking to each other, and the bell ringing on the door blended like a song. Finally, Nichole saw her parents sitting at a table in the back corner and pressed her way through the crowd to join them. She climbed up on her mother's lap.

"Did you find one you like?" Madge asked.

"Yes," Nichole answered, "It is chocolate, chocolate, and chocolate!"

"Of course!" Madge laughed.

They ended up waiting almost an hour longer while the morning crowd of customers shrunk down. At last, the man behind the counter came and sat down at the table next to them.

"Whew!" He exclaimed as he fell in the chair and stretched his legs out in front of him.

"Is it like that every morning?" Madge asked.

"Yes. Most of them are regulars," he answered, "I get here at 2:30 every morning to get ready for the morning rush."

"That is still nighttime!" Nichole exclaimed.

"Yes, it is," he chuckled.

After a momentary pause, Nichole asked, "Who is looney?"

He chuckled, "I am Mr. Looney."

"That is your name?" Nichole asked, baffled.

He chuckled, "That is right. Would you like a donut?" Nichole looked to her dad for approval.

"We don't have much money," Andy confessed.

"It's on me," Mr. Looney declared and motioned for Nichole to follow him. She looked to her dad once more and when he nodded, she climbed off her mother's lap and followed Mr. Looney to the glass case. He squatted down next to her and asked, "Which one would you like?" Nichole pointed to the chocolate donut with the chocolate frosting and chocolate sprinkles.

"Excellent choice," he declared, before standing and walking behind the counter. Using a small square of wax paper, he picked out the donut Nichole had selected and brought it around to her.

"Thank you," Nichole whispered overwhelmed by the kindness of this stranger. She took the donut, turned, and ran to scamper back up onto her mom's lap.

Nichole lifted the donut to her lips, and, before she took the first bite, the smell enveloped her to a chocolatey glee. She opened her mouth and sunk her teeth into the donut. Frosting pressed into her lips as she chewed, leaving a creamy brown ring around her entire mouth. "Mmmmm," she announced her approved with a mouthful of donut.

While Nichole enjoyed her donut, Mr. Looney and Andy spoke. Mr. Looney showed him a rack of newspapers that he sold to his customers each day. "I always have plenty of papers left at the end of the day if you would like to take them," Mr. Looney explained, "I know it is not much but you are welcome to it."

"Why do you want to help us?" Madge asked somewhat cautious.

Mr. Looney looked down at his feet before answering, "I know what it is like to fall on hard times and I know what it is like to have plenty. I would not be where I am now if someone had not given me a hand at some point," he explained.

"We really do appreciate it," Madge replied.

"It is not much but I know every little bit helps," he answered back. "Come back around 7:00 this evening, and whatever papers I have left are yours." He turned to Nichole as she popped the last piece of donuts into her mouth. "If I have any donuts left at the end of the day, you are welcome to them as well!" Nichole's eyes lit up.

Andy thanked Mr. Looney, shook his hand, and promised to come back that evening.

The family left the donut shop and got into their truck to leave. "I wonder if other businesses would do that," Andy considered. "Let's go and see!"

They pulled away in their truck and spent the rest of the morning driving to various donut shops and restaurants. Most places turned them away, but one Chinese restaurant manager told Andy if they came by on a certain night of the week, he would leave the leftover food in a hidden sealed bag beside their dumpster. He explained that his boss would not approve of him giving food away, so he would leave it there in a secret place for them. Andy thanked him. He had taken food from sealed containers straight out of dumpsters before, so a special container hidden outside of the dumpster was quite an improvement.

After visiting a few other businesses, they resumed their usual dumpster diving, and Nichole laced up her roller blades to race from dumpster to dumpster and help toss newspapers into the back of the truck. Sometimes Nichole would climb on top of a stack of newspapers, roller blades and all. Lifting herself up, she would lay her stomach across the side of the dumpster, with her head dangling inside the dumpster and her rollerbladed feet swinging in the air to balance her. Sometimes she would find toys, books, and even clothes.

After a long day of rollerblading and dumpster diving, they drove to the recycling yard to drop off their load, got paid, and then head back to the donut shop. Mr. Looney was saying goodbye to his final customer for the day when they arrived, and he told Andy to pull around to the back entrance while he locked up the front.

They pulled around to the back and noticed a stack of newspapers already placed outside the back door. As Andy was lifting them into the truck, Mr. Looney appeared. "Come on in!" He called out. Andy, Madge, and Nichole followed him through the door, which led to the enormous kitchen where they made the donuts. He directed them to a tall rack. The bottom shelves were empty but Mr. Looney reached up on one of the higher shelves and started pulling down donut after donut and placing them in a pink box. Nichole's eyes grew wide. Finally, Mr. Looney closed the box and handed it to Andy. "I cannot sell these tomorrow, so they are all yours."

Andy thanked him and then handed the box to Nichole. She wrapped her arms around the box as if something might try to steal them away from her. Andy and Mr. Looney shook hands and walked back out to the truck. "Thank you, Mr. Looney!" Nichole shouted as she climbed into the truck with her mom. Andy came around to the driver's side, and they drove away.

It was dark by now, so Andy drove further into the hills. He found a secluded road, where he backed the truck up near a tree so that the branches reached over the truck like a giant blanket. "I have an idea," Andy announced, and he climbed out of the truck and asked Madge to join him. Together they gathered all of the extra blankets that they had collected from dumpsters and spread them in the bed of the truck. "Finally, we can sleep lying down," he declared. "No one should bother us out here, so we do not need to be in the cab ready to leave so quickly."

Madge nodded her approval, and she rolled one of the blankets into a long pillow.

Meanwhile, in the cab of the truck, Nichole was enjoying a feast of donuts. When they first got the box, she had peeked inside and counted sixteen donuts! There were now only nine left. Madge came to the cab and lifted Nichole out and up into the bed of the truck. "What do you think of our bed tonight, Baby?" Madge asked. Nichole stood in the middle of the bed, looked around, and glanced up into the night sky. "It is beautiful, Mommy!"

Madge grinned as she climbed into the bed and pulled back a layer of blankets for them to crawl under. Nichole shimmied in next to Madge while Andy returned to the cab for one more heroin fix for the evening. Their addiction was requiring more and more use each day just to keep from getting sick, let alone to reach a good high. Coming off heroin was a fate so nearing death that they would do whatever they could to avoid it.

In their new bed, Madge and Nichole attempted to fall asleep. "Mommy, I am not sleepy yet," Nichole squirmed in the bed.

"Well, it is no wonder; you did eat a lot of donuts today," Madge replied.

"They were so yummy!" Nichole declared. "Can you tell me a bedtime story?"

Madge thought for a moment. "Okay," she began, "Once upon a time, there was a little girl named Nichole..."

Nichole giggled and chimed in, "Does she have a doggy?"

"Yes, she had a dog named..."

"Misty!" Nichole cried out, "Like the doggy I had when I was a baby."

"Okay, so she had a dog named Misty. One day Nichole was taking Misty for a walk on the beach..."

Nichole interrupted, "but Nichole helped at an animal hospital, so she got to play with lots of animals, right Mommy?"

"…Right, there was a veterinarian hospital near the beach. After helping take care of the animals, Nichole was taking her dog Misty for a walk."

"And then Nichole saw something moving out in the water!" Nichole added.

"She did?" Madge asked.

"Yeah, and Nichole watched, and she could tell it was not a bird because it kept going under water and coming back up."

"What was it?" Madge turned on her side to look at Nichole.

"Well, Nichole decided to swim out and see, because she was a good swimmer, and her dog sat on the beach and waited for her because she was a good dog. Then Nichole found out it was a little boy, and she rescued him and helped him swim back to the sand."

Madge grinned, "Nichole is very brave!"

"Yes, and then she helped him find his family because he was lost."

Madge listened as Nichole continued the story.

"And Nichole became his new friend. And his name was George. Nichole invited him to her house for dinner because she had a REALLY big house with a lot of rooms and lots of animals. And they had donuts for dinner, and then he went home with his family!"

"That is quite a bedtime story!" Madge declared.

Nichole giggled. "Then what happened, Mommy?" Nichole waited for her mom to finish the story.

"Then Nichole's mommy tucked her in her great big bed and said, 'Good night, Baby, I love you'."

Nichole smiled as her eyes started to drift closed, "Good night, Mommy. I love you too."

From the front seat, Andy had begun to come out of his daze. "What about me?"

"Oh, you were there too, Daddy!" Nichole giggled as she cuddled close to her mom.

Finally, Andy climbed into the bed in the truck and crawled under the blankets. Snuggled between her parents with the stars shimmering overhead, Nichole drifted to sleep. Andy nodded to sleep aided by the high from his last hit of heroin. Madge tried to fall asleep while she stared at the stars overhead, but she heard a coyote howl in the distance and every single sway of a tree branch would alert her. She slept off and on all through the night.

CHAPTER 6

By the time the sun peaked over the horizon, Madge had been awake for hours. She looked around the truck to make sure the coast was clear and then climbed out to go behind the tree to go to the bathroom. By the time she climbed back in the truck, Andy had woken up. He groaned, stretched, and then laid there for a few minutes as his eyes adjusted to the daylight. He then climbed out of the truck, took a deep breath, and coughed from deep in his throat.

"We cannot sleep here again," Madge announced.

"Why?" Andy rubbed his eyes as he looked around them.

"There was a coyote walking around our truck last night is why!" she answered.

"How do you know that?" Andy lit a cigarette and took a deep puff.

"Because I could not sleep, and I saw it," She explained.

Andy walked around the truck, "Hey! You are right. Look over here!" He kneeled down and pointed to some tracks on the ground. Cool!"

"That is not okay!" Madge exclaimed, "We cannot sleep out here where we could be eaten by a coyote!"

Andy chuckled and nodded as he finished his cigarette. Madge turned to Nichole who was still sleeping in the truck. She wiped Nichole's tangled brown hair out of her eyes. Nichole stirred and tried to lift the blankets over her eyes to block out the sunlight.

"It's morning, Baby. Time to wake up!" Madge tugged the blankets back.

"Is it time for school?" Nichole asked.

"No, Baby, you aren't in school anymore," Madge whispered and cast a stern look towards Andy.

He heard her response and called back, "We will take her to school tomorrow."

Madge didn't pay any attention to his empty promise.

"Oh, yeah," Nichole started to wake up and remembered where they were. "What are we doing today?"

"We need to get a good load of newspapers today. We lost a lot of time yesterday at the donut shop and checking all of the other businesses," Andy walked back to the truck and dropped his cigarette in the ashtray and tapped the end until it stopped burning. He then returned the cigarette stub to its box.

"Can I eat some donuts now?" Nichole jumped out of the blankets suddenly wide awake. Madge laughed as Nichole jumped out of the back of the truck and in the front where the donuts waited.

Madge folded the blankets into tight bundles and arranged them so they could fit behind their seat, leaving the bed of the truck for the newspapers they would gather that day. By the time she finished putting the blankets away Nichole had already finished her first donut.

As soon as they were all settled in the truck, Andy headed out on a route for the businesses that they had visited the day before. At a few of the stops, they were able to collect some of the day-old newspapers. Once he completed the circuit of businesses, they returned to their regular route of apartment complexes and condos.

Before they knew it, the bed of the truck was brimming with newspapers. For the first time, they were able to beat the end-of-the-day crowd at the recycling center. In fact, there was not even a line when Andy pulled onto the large scale. Since they went to the same recycling center every single time, the workers had gotten to know them.

Thanks to her donuts for breakfast, Nichole was more hyper than usual and decided to play while her parents unloaded the truck. Jumping out of her seat, she scanned the area for something fun to do.

She considered putting on her roller blades, but there were too many tractors and trucks between the piles of different types of paper to go far. Nichole turned and looked at the brimming piles of newspapers where her parents were unloading their truck. Parts of the pile were taller than a small building. To Nichole's young eyes, it looked like a mountain that needed an explorer to conquer it. She walked passed her parents who had not realized that she got out of the truck and began her climb taking careful steps onto the first small mound of papers. Some of the sections of paper shifted under her shoes and she had to reposition her feet to keep standing. Taking a few more unsteady steps up, she then heard her mother yell from behind her, "Be careful!"

Nichole looked back and waved to show her mom that she heard her warning. Across the recycling yard, a few of the employees saw

Nichole and they were keeping a watchful eye on her. She climbed up a little further until she reached a low peak. It was not the top, but she decided by the look on her mother's face that this was as far as she dared explore without causing her mother to faint from fright. She turned to look all around. She could see the entire recycling center. Satisfied with her brave accomplishment, Nichole crouched down until she was sitting on the newsprint with her feet tucked in front of her. Sliding, she made her way down to the bottom.

Madge was waiting for her at the bottom, "You scared me half to death!" She scolded. "There could have been a hole in the pile, and you could have fallen in and been buried by tons of paper!"

"I am sorry, Mommy," Nichole looked down at her feet. She hated to see her mother worry. "I will not ever do it again."

"Oh, my baby," Madge reached for her and hugged her close, "I do not mean to get upset, but you are the most important person in my life, and I could not bear for anything to happen to you!"

Nichole squeezed her mother back and promised never to cause her to worry again.

They got back in the truck and continued on the second route of dumpster diving since there was still had time left in the day.

They took a break for lunch at McDonald's, and while Nichole played in the tunnels and ball pit of the play area, her parents parked the truck in the most secluded part of the parking lot to get their fix for the day. Madge took a larger hit than usual that day to calm her frazzled nerves.

Finally, they finished their hit and went inside to watch Nichole play for a few more minutes. They then decided to leave to find a new place to park for the night. Parking in the hills again was out of the question since the coyote scare from the night before.

Finally, they settled on a dark street with a few houses on it. Since it was where people might notice them, they decided not to sleep in the back or else they would draw too much attention to themselves and would not be able to leave quickly if they had to.

Madge took out just one blanket from behind the seat and stretched it across them. The weather was a little warmer, so they did not need the thick pile of blankets that they usually used. Andy and Madge rested their heads against their windows and Nichole stretched across their laps. After such a long day of gathering two loads for recycling, they all drifted to sleep without another word.

"Rap, Rap, Rap" a pounding knock on the window woke Andy and Madge with a jolt. A man in a suit was pounding on Andy's window.

"You cannot sleep here!" The man yelled.

Andy looked around them. The sun had not even begun to rise. It was still the middle of the night! Nichole woke but was too frightened to get up, so she peeked one of her eyes out of the blankets and saw the man's angry face. 'What was wrong with sleeping?' Nichole wondered. 'We are not bothering anyone.'

Andy considered giving the man a piece of his mind, but thought better of it and turned the key in the ignition, shifted into drive, and sped away. He spent the rest of the night driving from one street to another, only staying a few minutes before moving on. By the time the sun began to reveal itself, they had been awake for several hours. Finally, Andy pulled into a gas station and used some of the money they had left from the day before to fill up the gas tank. He also bought two bottles of chocolate milk, a king size Reese's peanut butter cup, and a bag of beef jerky for their breakfast.

While they were sitting in the parking lot eating their breakfast, a police car pulled into the lot and cruised up and down the aisles. Immediately, Andy sprang in action tidying up their truck and hiding all of the drug paraphernalia. "We cannot do anything to draw attention to ourselves!" He instructed Madge and Nichole. "If the police have no reason to stop us or talk to us, then we will be fine." He faked a calm composure, almost holding his breath until the police car left the parking lot. He let out a heavy sign, and his hands trembled from the adrenaline it took to hold himself together. He peered all around them to make sure no one else was watching.

Opening his door, he stepped out and signaled for Nichole to follow him. "Our registration has expired! We cannot have a cop pulling us over for a small violation like that and then finding drugs on us." Andy walked through the parking lot with Nichole while Madge cleaned up the trash that had collected in the truck. Finally, Andy stopped behind a car with a sticker on the license plate that read 1995. "Keep a lookout and let me know if anyone is around," Andy commanded. Nichole stood by her dad and looked all around them to make sure the coast was clear while he squatted behind the car. Using his keys, he scraped the sticker off the license plate, being careful not to let it tear or leave any piece behind. At last, he managed to get the sticker off in one whole piece and sprang to his feet like a jack in the box. He looked all around them before taking Nichole's hand and walking back to their truck. Again, he asked her to keep watch while he put the sticker on their license plate, being careful to make sure it stuck. With the task completed, they climbed back in the truck and cruised away.

At one dumpster, Nichole spotted a snail crawling on the sidewalk nearby. The snail's shell was weathered and peeling, and Nichole determined that the snail must be very old and needed somebody to look after it. Looking around, she spotted a cardboard shoebox that her dad had pulled from the trash to recycle. She grabbed the box and bent down to pick up the snail with her fingertips. She set it in the box and plucked some grass from the lawn and leaves from a bush.

Nichole sprinkled grass and leaves inside the box and carried it to the truck. She climbed onto her seat where she waited for her parents to join her. After a few minutes, they joined her back in the truck.

Immediately Madge noticed the box and asked," What is in there?"

Nichole held out the box for her mom to see her new pet. "His name is Oldie!" Nichole announced. This was not the first creature that Nichole had rescued. Ever since she was a toddler, she had been saving snails, frogs, and any creature that she could.

For days, Nichole carried Oldie and his box everywhere with her. One day while they were out dumpster diving, Nichole set the box on the side ledge of the truck while she explored. The dumpster did not have much to offer, so the family all piled back into the truck and started to pull away.

Nichole looked all around herself in a panic, "Where is Oldie?"

At that exactly same moment, they all heard a crunch as the truck rolled forward a few feet. Andy and Madge looked at each other, knowing what had just happened.

Nichole climbed over Andy's lap and let herself out to look for her pet snail. There, smashed under the truck tire was Oldie, box and all. Nichole burst into tears and fell to her knees. Andy gathered her up in his arms and placed her back in the truck. Madge held Nichole, trying to console her broken heart, as Andy drove the truck away slowly.

CHAPTER 7

As was their daily routine, Andy, Madge, and Nichole woke early. They made their rounds through different communities to scavenge the dumpsters. By this point, they had learned the trash pickup schedules. Knowing where to go the day before trash pickup, they got larger loads within shorter amounts of time.

They even found ways to change the full and empty weights of their truck when they took it to the recycling center. One con that they used was for Nichole to hide under a blanket while they drove through the scale with a full truck. When they drove back around for the empty weight, she snuck out and hid behind a building, where she waited for them to finish.

Another con they used was to go to a self-service car wash and wet the newspapers before putting another layer of dry newspapers on top. This con worked one time when a new worker was operating the scale. He did not realize that the full weight was far too high to be realistic.

One afternoon, while Andy and Madge were dumpster diving and Nichole was rollerblading, a man came out of his apartment. He slammed his door so hard the building shook and he began screaming and running toward them. Nichole looked around to see where the noise was coming from. When she saw the man racing toward her, she pivoted in her roller blades, lost her balance and fell onto her back. The man continued to advance toward them. "Get away from here, you dirty pieces of trash!" Andy jumped out of the dumpster where he had been passing things to Madge for her to toss into the truck. "You heard me, you junkies!" The man continued, "You are disgusting, and you cannot be here. That is city property."

Madge ran to where Nichole was scrambling on her hands and knees to get into the truck. She scooped her up in her arms, lifted her into the truck in one fluid motion. She slammed and locked the door behind them. Andy stood up to the angry young man, trying to defend his family. "We are not hurting anyone; we're just trying to get by." The man just yelled louder. Finally, Andy screamed and cursed back until the man backed off. Andy walked passed him and climbed into the truck with his family. He signaled his middle finger at the man and sped away.

Nichole's body shook with inconsolable sobs and her hands bled from small scratches with small pebbles buried in them. Her tailbone throbbed from where she had fallen on it. More than the physical pain, she felt fear. Never before had somebody yelled at them and chased them away. She struggled to catch her breath, and Madge rocked her in her arms attempting to comfort her. Her sobs turned in hiccups, and she continued to shudder and cry for over an hour.

Andy was in a fit of rage at the way the man had treated them, especially seeing how frightened his daughter was. Once Nichole composed herself, Andy dropped Madge and Nichole off at McDonalds for dinner, and then he got back into the truck and drove away. The sun had set, so using the cover of darkness he drove back to the same neighborhood.

He turned off his headlights as he neared where the man lived. He parked a short distance away and crept to the carport where the guy parked his car. Andy's heart pounded in his chest as he crept up next to the car. He looked around to make sure nobody was watching. Slipping his keys out from his pocket, he gripped one key in his fist and jabbed it into the side of the car. With a few quick breaths, he lunged forward and ran around the car digging the key into the metal. The groaning screech of the scratching metal echoed in the carport.

When he completed his lap around the car, he bounded back to his truck before anyone could catch him. He scampered into his seat and slammed the door before speeding away not bothering to turn on his headlights until he was half a block away. Alone on the open road knowing he had gotten away with his revenge, he laughed with a victorious confidence to himself. He screamed out the window "Take that..." He trailed off with a long list of profanity.

At last, he arrived back at the McDonald's, where Madge and Nichole were waiting. They climbed in the truck, and Madge looked at Andy and saw that he had beads of sweat streaming from his brow. "What did you do?" She asked with dread in her voice.

Andy laughed again, "I just keyed his car! It's nothing compared to what he deserved."

Andy pulled to a stop on a dark street, and Nichole turned in her seat looking around them. "What if somebody finds us?" She asked wide-eyed, remembering how the man had woke them that morning.

"There are no houses on this street." Andy pointed out, "Nobody will bother us."

"What will we do tomorrow, Daddy?" Nichole looked up at her dad.

"What do you mean? We'll do what we always do." He answered with a shrug of his shoulders.

Nichole began to quiver and shake. "Please, Daddy! Please don't make us go dumpster diving again!" Giant tears streaked her face.

Momentary frustration came over Andy at this daughter's emotion until he looked at her face and saw the terror in her eyes. Madge stroked Nichole's hair, and Nichole crawled onto her lap, where she curled up into a shivering ball.

"Oh, man!" Andy grumbled, knowing he would not force his daughter to go dumpster diving after what they had just experienced. "I will figure something out. We don't have to go dumpster diving tomorrow."

Nichole calmed herself by stroking the hem of her shirt between two of her fingers. Despite her attempts, she continued to shake and sniffle until she fell asleep in Madge's arms. Once she was asleep, Madge helped her lie down on the seat between them so that they could have a hit of heroin before going to sleep.

While Andy prepared the black tar on the foil, Madge asked him, "What are we going to do now?"

"I don't know!" Andy answered as he took his first hit. They both took a longer hit than usual, completely emptying their stash.

CHAPTER 8

The next morning Andy squinted as the sun rose. He had not slept very well the night before knowing that he needed to figure out another way to make money. After seeing the terror in his daughter's eyes, he and Madge both knew that could not take her out dumpster diving with them again.

He turned on the truck, and Madge started to wake. Nichole continued sleeping deeply between them. She had sobbed and shuddered in her sleep through most of the night. Nichole's tossing and turning were part of the reason that Andy had a difficult time sleeping very well.

Madge looked down at Nichole's head on her lap. Dirt and tearstains left zigzags across Nichole's face. Andy drove down the road without any destination in mind. Madge turned to Andy, "We need to wash up. We need to find a bathroom or something." She motioned to Nichole's messy face.

Andy continued to drive without saying anything in return. Madge ran her fingers through Nichole's hair separating the tangles bit by bit.

After an hour of driving around, Andy got an idea and pointed the truck toward the local train station. They had large bathrooms, and people are always coming and going, so they should not draw much attention to themselves there.

Andy pulled into the parking lot and positioned the truck in the furthest section of the lot where few other cars bothered to park. When they came to a stop, Nichole moaned, stretched, and then her eyes fluttered open. All of the crying from the day before left her eyes red and puffy. Madge helped her put on her shoes and tied the laces while Nichole ate a handful of beef jerky left from the day before.

Once they were ready, Madge took Nichole's hand and together they walked into the train station. After going to the bathroom and washing their hands they waited for any other women to leave so that they were alone, Madge grabbed a handful of paper towels and wet them under the faucet. She wiped Nichole's face, arms, and legs, using several wet towels, as the layers of dirt soiled each one.

While Madge and Nichole washed up, Andy strolled through the station until he spotted a newspaper rack next to one of the doors. He saw Madge and Nichole come out of the women's restroom and nodded to Madge for her to take Nichole to the car. He followed several yards behind them, and, as he approached the exit, he approached a newspaper stand; he swiped the top paper from the stand and shoved it in his jacket. He quickened his pace, still trying to appear casual. He opened the door and stepped outside without anybody noticing that he did not pay for the paper.

With his long legs, Andy was able to walk and still catch up to Madge and Nichole. Nichole turned to see her dad walking beside her and reaching up, she grabbed his hand, while her other hand held her mother's hand. "Swing me," Nichole asked. Andy and Madge looked at each other. He tucked his newspaper under his free arm and together they lunged forward and lifted their arms high, swinging Nichole in the air. Nichole laughed loudly as she landed back on the ground.

Back at the truck, Andy plopped into the driver's seat, leaving the door open, and pulled out the first section of the newspaper. Madge and Nichole never understood his fascination with the news but he tried to read the newspaper every single day.

Seeing that they were going to stay there for a while, Madge got an idea. "Come here, Baby," she signaled to Nichole. Early the day before, Madge had found a Frisbee in one of the dumpsters. She pulled it out from under her seat and handed it to Nichole. "A Frisbee!" Nichole exclaimed. "Can we play?"

Looking around the parking lot, Madge found a large area where nobody else had parked. She motioned for Nichole to follow her. Nichole had never thrown a Frisbee before, so Madge showed her how to hold it with her fingers and then curl her arm to her chest. Standing behind her, Madge maneuvered Nichole's arms to show the motion of unfurling the Frisbee from her grasp. After giving her step-by-step instruction, Madge jogged a few yards in front of Nichole in order to catch the Frisbee.

Nichole concentrated on her mom's instructions. Holding the Frisbee across her chest, she flung her arm out. The Frisbee flew through the air, circling around Nichole and landing several yards behind her, nearly hitting a car. Nichole ducked down, slapped her hands over her mouth, and her eyes grew wide. Madge looked around to make sure the owner of the car was not around and then laughed as she ran to Nichole. "It's okay, Baby. You will get used to it." Madge ran her fingers through Nichole's hair.

Running to where the Frisbee landed, Madge retrieved it and took it back to where they were playing. This time, Madge decided to do the first toss. She did each motion slowly so that Nichole would be ready. She twisted her body to the side and wrapped the Frisbee around herself, swung her arm around, and released it so that it landed near Nichole's feet. Nichole jumped up and down clapping, "You did it, Mommy!"

"Thank you, Baby. Now it is your turn," Madge answered.

Nichole bent over and picked up the Frisbee. Again, trying to recreate the movements her mom had shown, her she whipped the Frisbee a little more slowly this time and it flew high in the air and came back, spinning to the ground a short distance in front of Nichole. "See, you are getting better," Madge called out as she ran forward and picked up the Frisbee off the ground. "Now let's see if you can catch it." Standing just out of arm's reach from Nichole, she tossed the Frisbee forward, and Nichole clapped her hands together as the Frisbee slipped through them. They repeated this exercise until Nichole mastered clasping the flying Frisbee between both of her hands. They continued to play for several hours until Nichole had learned to throw and catch the Frisbee. While they played, Andy read his newspaper, trying to come up with a plan for the next day, and finally, he decided to take a nap.

Finally, Madge and Nichole returned to the truck, where Andy was snoring loudly with his newspaper sprawled across his lap. At the sound of Madge and Nichole returning to the truck, he jerked awake. Nichole giggled at his reaction, but he looked quite distressed for a moment until he looked around himself and saw that he was just in the truck with his family and not under some sort of attack.

He mumbled something to himself, and they looked up, "How was the Frisbee?"

Nichole lit up, "It was so much fun! Mommy showed me how to throw it and catch it, and I got really good. Didn't I, Mommy?" Nichole looked up at Madge expectantly.

"Yes, you did," Madge answered stroking a wisp of hair out of Nichole's face.

"Good...good," Andy replied as he trailed off into a daydream. He returned to the present with a start, "Oh! I have to tell you something. I have an idea for how we can get some money."

Nichole did not like talking about money so she found her bucket of beads and climbed through the small back window leading to the bed of the truck, where she could play while her parents talked.

"Really?" Madge asked waiting for his solution.

"Well, not money exactly...A kind of money," Andy rambled.

"What are you talking about?"

"Remember, before we had to move out? Your application for food stamps was approved. You used my parent's address." Andy stared at her as if the answer was so obvious.

"So what? You will not go to your parents for help." Madge reminded him.

"But they have our mail. We just have to figure out a way to get it without them knowing." Andy acted as though this was the simplest request he had ever made.

"And how exactly do you plan to do that?" Madge prodded.

"We just need to go during the day while everyone is at work. I am sure I can find a window to get in. We can sneak in, grab our mail, and leave." Andy tossed his hands in the air as though he had come up with the most brilliant plan.

"And if someone sees us and calls the cops?" Madge pointed out.

"We are not stealing! We are going to get what is rightfully ours." Andy dismissed her concern.

"We cannot do this now. It is already afternoon. They will already be getting home."

"Exactly! We will go tomorrow!" Andy folded his arms across his chest and grinned.

Madge shook her head, hating that she was living this way, but not knowing any other options. "Well, we better get some good sleep tonight if you expect us to pull this off."

"Obviously!" Andy answered as if he was the one who said it. He shifted in his seat and turned the truck on, ready to shift into gear.

"Slow down!" Madge scolded and called for Nichole to come back into the front seat so they could go.

"I was not leaving," Andy claimed, "Just getting ready."

Nichole slid her narrow frame through the small sliding window, twisted around in the seat, and buckled her seatbelt.

Now Andy shifted the truck into gear and pulled out of the train station parking lot. Finding a quiet park that had no street lights, they pulled into a spot where the shadows hid them from view.

Madge pulled out their growing supply of blankets and spread them across, with Andy and Madge sleeping in a seated position, heads resting on the windows, and Nichole burrowed between them.

CHAPTER 9

Nichole woke to find them still parked in the same place they had been when she fell asleep. She stretched and yawned before sitting up. Her dad was not in the truck, but her mom was sitting next to her and noticed when she sat up. "Good morning, Baby." "Good morning, Mommy."

Andy had walked across the street to the convenience store to buy a newspaper for a quarter and chocolate milk. When he got back, he climbed into the driver's seat and set his newspaper on the dash. The previous day's paper lay sprawled under Madge and Nichole's feet.

"So what are we going to do today?" Madge asked.

"I told you yesterday what my plan was," He answers calmly.

"I did not think you were serious," Madge replied.

"Of course, I am serious! It is our food stamps, and we should have them."

Nichole looked back and forth at her parents. "Where are we going to get food stamps?" Nichole asked.

"At your Granny and Grandpa's," Andy announced.

"Good. I miss them," Nichole shared for the first time.

"You are not going to get to see them," Madge pointed out.

"Why not?" Nichole whined.

Andy turned his body so he was facing them with one knee propped on the seat. He began to explain, "We are going to go when nobody is home and sneak in."

Nichole dropped her shoulders, "Oh."

Andy shook his head, surprised that they did not appreciate his brilliant idea. He started up the truck and pulled out of the parking lot.

He first drove to their drug connection, knowing that they could not risk suffering withdrawals while breaking in. They also needed to stall to make sure that everybody was gone to work before they arrived. After Andy made the drug pick up, they parked on a secluded street and had their fix while Nichole played with her beads in the back of the truck. This had become their only ritual that created any consistency in Nichole's life.

After waiting a few hours and confident that everybody should be working by now, they began the drive back to Andy's parents' house. They drove up in the hill communities and turned down the long road, which also led to their former home. At the crossroads, one direction would take them back to the house they had fled from in the middle of the night, and the other pointed in his parents' driveway. Andy turned left into the long driveway. He drove to the end and parked. Just as

Andy had planned it, there were no cars, which meant nobody was home.

"Wait here for a second," Andy whispered as he slipped out of the truck to run around the property and see if anybody was around. After a couple minutes, he returned panting. "It is all clear. No one is around."

"I am not doing this," Madge protested.

Andy heaved a heavy sigh. "Fine. Then stay here and be the lookout."

Andy climbed back out of the truck and slipped around the side of the house. He checked all of the doors and windows, but every single lock was secure. While he was checking the doors, a dog started running back and forth in the house. It was his sister's dog Zamu, a tan and white Basenji. He waited and breathed a sigh of relief when he remembered that Basenjis do not bark. However, seeing the dog gave him an idea. He went around checking for a doggy door. In the backyard, he found the doggy door. Squatting down on his hands and knees, he checked the door. There was no way that he could fit through it. His shoulders were too broad. But then he got a new idea. He jogged back to the truck where Madge and Nichole were waiting.

"Did you get it?" Madge asked.

"No," he replied, "the doors and windows are locked, but there is a doggy door."

"Can you fit?" Madge asked.

"No, but Nichole could," He answered.

Madge rolled her eyes, knowing she would not be able to talk him out of it.

Taking Nichole by the hand then, he walked her around the house and showed her the doggy door. "All you have to do is crawl inside and unlock the door for me," Andy explained.

Nichole got down on her hands and knees and pushed her head through the flap. There staring at her from across the room was Zamu. "Hi, Zamu," Nichole called out hoping she remembered her. "Are you a good girl?" Nichole wriggled her way through the door as Zamu paced and pranced back and forth unsure of whether to attack the intruder or to play with her. Finally, Nichole pulled her feet through the tiny door and stood up. Behind her Andy tapped on the sliding glass door and pointed to the lock. Nichole unclipped the lock holding the door closed, and Andy slid it open. Zamu became more frantic since there were two intruders in her home, but she kept a careful distance.

Nichole remembered coming over after school before they had been homeless. She used to play with Zamu, so she tried to get her to calm down. Walking in the kitchen, Nichole checked the pantry for doggy treats and found a bag on the top shelf. Using each shelf like a ladder, Nichole pulled herself up and used one hand to knock the treats off the edge. The bag bounced off Nichole's head before landing on the floor. "Ouch," She muttered even though it did not really hurt. She climbed back down and removed one treat from the bag. She then gripped the top of the bag between her lips and climbed back up to put it away hoping that nobody would be able to tell that she had been there. With the bag set back on the shelf, Nichole jumped to the ground with a thud. "What are you doing?" Andy called out.

"I am getting a treat for Zamu!" Nichole shouted back.

Picking up the dog treat off the floor, Nichole walked back to the living room where Zamu was watching Andy, trying to decide if he was a friend or enemy. Andy was rummaging through a pile of mail on the kitchen counter.

Nichole started walking slowly toward Zamu. Zamu backed away, ready to run and hide until Nichole bent down on her knees and stretched her hand out with the treat in it. Zamu paused, stretched her neck out without moving her feet any closer, and sniffed the air. "That's right Zamu. I have a treat for you. Do you want a TREAT?" Nichole called out in a soft singsong voice. Zamu would not budge, so Nichole slowly inched forward on her knees with the treat in her hand.

All of the while Andy was digging through the pile of mail and paperwork trying to find anything with Madge's name on it.

At last, Nichole got close enough where Zamu could reach the treat from her hand, and, before allowing her to take it, Nichole ran her hand along Zamu's back twice and then released the treat. Zamu gently picked up the treat with her teeth and laid down to gnaw on it. Nichole cuddled up next to her and stroked her back. When Zamu finished the treat, she sprang to her feet. "Do you want to play?" Nichole asked, still squatted next to her. Zamu pounded her paws on the carpet to show that she did want to play. Nichole stood to her feet and ran around the house with Zamu, while Andy continued to search through the mail.

"Ha! I got it!" Andy announced as he lifted an envelope in the air. Nichole turned and ran back in the dining room to see. "These are our food stamps," Andy showed the envelope to Nichole. "Now we will have to get out of here!"

Nichole walked back to where Zamu sat, waiting to play some more. "We have to go, Zamu. You be a good girl," Nichole sat down in front of the dog and wrapped her arms around its neck.

"Hurry, let's go!" Andy called out while standing at the sliding glass door. "You need to lock the door behind me."

Nichole came running, and, after Andy slid the door closed, Nichole lifted the latch, locking it in place. She then bent down and crawled back out through the doggy door. This time Zamu followed her out, and

Nichole rubbed her back and gave her one more hug before following her dad out the gate and back to the truck.

Climbing back in the truck, Andy tossed the envelope on Madge's lap. "See! I told you it would work." His grin stretched across his face.

"And I got to play with Zamu, and I gave her a treat!" Nichole shared. "I wish I had a pet and not just a snail, like Oldie."

Her mother smiled and stroked Nichole's hair.

Andy backed the truck out of the parking space and drove down the long driveway and back onto the main road.

Madge turned the envelope over in her hands before finally sliding her finger under the flap and tearing it open. Inside were small packets of food stamps with different numbers to show how much they were worth. Madge opened one packet and gently torn one off along the perforated edge. "So what are we going to buy with these?" Madge asked, "It is not like we can buy anything that needs to be refrigerated or cooked."

"We can get some snacks," Andy suggested.

After driving for a few miles, Andy pulled in a grocery store parking lot. "Let's get some dinner." He shifted the truck into park.

Together they all walked into the grocery store and picked out two bottles of chocolate milk for Andy and Nichole, a Diet Coke for Madge, a bag of beef jerky, and a pack of crumb donuts. At the checkout, Madge counted out the food stamps to pay for the food. The cashier gave her a one-dollar slip in food stamps for change. Walking out of the store, Andy complained, "We need to find us a place that gives real change instead of more food stamps."

"Where would we do that?" Madge asked, "I am sure all of the stores have food stamps."

"I will ask my new dealer. He probably knows where we can sell some of them," Andy thought aloud.

Andy found a pay phone outside of the store and walked over to call his dealer, while Madge and Nichole returned to the truck. A few minutes later, he joined them in the truck. "He said that he just got a fresh supply, and, if we come right now, he will give us a good deal." Andy looked over his shoulder before backing out of the parking space.

"Did he say anything about the food stamps?" Madge asked.

"Huh? Oh, I forgot to ask. I will ask him when we get there," Andy answered.

He sped out of the parking lot and headed for the drug dealer's pick up spot. During the drive, they each enjoyed their drinks, and Madge and Nichole shared the beef jerky, while Andy devoured the crumb donuts.

Finally, they arrived at the alley behind the house where the dealer agreed to meet them. Andy parked the truck along the side of the alley and went to the back door. He rapped on the door several times before someone answered. Before making the exchange of cash for drugs, Andy asked him whether he knew of anybody interested in buying food stamps. The dealer asked some of the other people inside the house. Someone shared that there was a produce truck nearby that accepted food stamps and gave back cash for change. Andy thanked them, made the exchange, and ran back to the truck.

"What did he say?" Madge asked.

"There is a produce truck that takes food stamps but gives change in cash just down the street," Andy answered.

Andy pulled the truck out of the alley and drove up and down the small streets until he spotted the produce truck parked on the side of the road.

"There it is," he pointed as he pulled the truck to the side of the road behind it.

The truck was tall, and the back doors swung wide-open revealing food and snacks hanging from the walls and ceiling as well as in boxes lining either side, with a small path in between. There was already a small line of people gathered inside the truck. Andy, Madge, and Nichole approached the back of the truck. In front of the rear bumper, a small folding stepladder was positioned to make it easier to climb up in the back of the massive truck.

Andy climbed in first, Madge helped Nichole up the ladder and then Andy pulled her up behind him. Lastly, Madge ascended the ladder and the family gazed all around them at the foods to choose from. There were boxes of fruits and vegetables, spicy Mexican candies, small bags of potato chips in every single flavor. On the ceiling above their heads, there were even piñatas dangling.

Andy picked up some chicken and shrimp flavored cup of noodles that they could heat up at a 7-Eleven, Madge chose some apples and a bunch of grapes, and Nichole picked out a bag of Cheetos and a king size Reese's candy bar. They worked their way to the front of the truck where the cashier/driver was waiting.

They each stood in line with their own items and the amount in food stamps to cover the cost and still return a reasonable amount of cash change. One by one, they made their purchase, and each time the cashier provided cash change in return. They squeezed past the other shoppers in the produce truck to return to their own vehicle. Once inside they counted their total change together. It came to a total of nearly ten dollars.

"It is not much," Andy counted out the coins and bills in his hand, "but it is still something."

"You know this is not going to be enough to get us by each day, do not you?" Madge asked.

"Yes, I know. I will figure something out." Andy rubbed the back of his neck and stared at the ceiling.

Once again, it was the end of another day. Andy drove the truck to an empty business parking lot and parked in the back. While Nichole ate her Cheetos and Reese's, Andy and Madge had their fix for the day. For the first time in a while, they all fell asleep with full stomachs, even if their meal was not the most nutritious.

Just as Andy and Madge were putting away the foil and lighter from their drug fix, a light flashed in the window. Andy jumped in his seat. The light flashed away and a security guard was standing at the driver's window. The security guard called out, "This is a place of business. No after-hours parking." Relieved that it was not an actual police officer, Andy just nodded and turned on the truck and drove away to find another place for them to settle in for the night.

CHAPTER 10

Andy coasted up and down the community streets scouting for a place to park and sleep for the night.

"We need to find a regular place to park at night where nobody will bother us," Madge rubbed her fingers over her forehead.

"I know this has gotten real old," Andy mumbled.

Every single street they drive down had homes or places of business.

"We could park in the hills again," Andy suggested.

"No!" Madge exclaimed. "There are coyotes out there."

Andy chuckled at her distress.

He made a left turn in another street lined with houses.

"Look out, Daddy!" Nichole yelled.

"What?" He slammed on the brakes.

Sitting in the middle of the road sat a brown and white rabbit staring into their headlights. Its ears stood straight up and its brown eyes reflected back the light from the headlights.

"It is a bunny!" Nichole unbuckled her seatbelt and leaned up against the dashboard to get a better look. "Can I have it?" Nichole spun around to face Andy.

He paused for a moment before answering. "You know what? Yes, you can." He answered.

"Yay!" Nichole bounced in her seat while Andy left the truck stopped in the middle of the street and then he slowly opened his door. At the noise and change in movement, the rabbit darted across the road. Andy sprang to action and ran after the rabbit.

The sun had already set, and the only light on the street came from a few porch lights. Nichole slid in Andy's seat and watched him chase the rabbit. Madge laughed at the desperate chase the rabbit was taking him on.

The rabbit ran across someone's lawn, and Andy followed gradually closing the distance. The rabbit darted under a bush in the next yard. Andy leaped over the bush, fell forward and caught himself with his hands braced underneath his chest. He scampered back to his feet, back in hot pursuit. The rabbit darted back across the street, and Andy sprinted behind it.

The next lawn had a trampoline set up in the yard, and the rabbit raced under it. More determined than ever, Andy crouched down and half ran, half crawled under the trampoline.

The rabbit darted in a zigzag trying to lose its pursuer. Andy cleared the trampoline and stood back to his full height. He looked around to spot which direction the rabbit ended up. Several yards ahead, it was crouching beside a brick wall and a garage. Slowly Andy crept closer.

The rabbit attempted to run past him and Andy skipped to the side, blocking it. It then turned back around facing the wall. Andy inched forward until he cowered over the rabbit. The rabbit froze as it realized it had nowhere to run.

He knew that if he attempted to grab it with his hands, it could escape, so he rapidly slipped his shirt over his head. In one smooth motion as soon as the shirt was off, he dropped it over the rabbit and braced it with his hands and knees. The rabbit squirmed violently, but Andy held his shirt tighter and leaned over, bracing his forearms across the wiggling shirt.

Gradually the rabbit slowed and, at last, stood still. Andy could still see it heaving with each breath. He eased his grip making sure that the rabbit did not try to escape, and then slid his hands across the shirt until they gripped the rabbit. His picked up the rabbit and wrapped the sides of the shirt around it like a sack. The rabbit started to wiggle and fight again, but Andy held the shirt tight and lifted it high in the air to make sure the rabbit did not bite or scratch him.

At last he had a chance to catch his breath and he realized that he had been heaving as heavily as the rabbit. Holding the t-shirt sack with one fist, he used his free hand to wipe away the sweat that streamed down his forehead into his eyes. He looked around to see if anybody had witnessed the chase, and all he could see has Nichole and Madge in the truck. Nichole was bouncing up and down and clapping once she realized that he had caught it.

Switching hands, he carried the rabbit back to the truck. Nichole rushed to open the door as he approached. He held up the squirming shirt. "You got it!" Nichole screamed with glee. She crawled backward across the seat to make room for Andy. He slid into his seat, holding the shirt and rabbit above his chest.

Nichole squirmed in her seat and giggled, anxious to meet her new pet. Andy slowly lowered the shirt it the floor, "Pull your feet up on the seat.

It is going to come out running." He cautioned. Nichole sat crouched on the seat, and Madge shifted to tuck her legs up under her. Andy turned sideways holding the shirt on the floor but not releasing just yet. He pulled his legs up and slowly released his grip on the shirt. Immediately the rabbit raced out and ran to the passenger side floorboard. Its ears twitched as it looked from side to side before darting back across the floor. Realizing that it had nowhere else to go, it attempted to dig its way under the seat.

"Oh, no, you don't!" Andy stuck his foot in the way to block it. He reached down and gripped the rabbit by the loose skin on the back of its neck.

"Don't hurt it, Daddy!" Nichole cried.

"I am not hurting it!" Andy answered and used his other hand to scoop up the rabbit and held its bottom feet together as it tried to kick free. He then moved his hand from the back of its neck to holding its front feet together. He tucked the back of the rabbit to his chest to hold it securely until it stopped trying to escape. He could feel its heart pounding against its tiny chest.

"Aw, it is so scared," Nichole whimpered.

"Yeah, it took me on quite a chase." Andy wiped away some of the sweat from his face. "Just give it a few minutes to calm down and then we can try to get it used to us."

While Andy held onto it, Nichole leaned forward and stroked the top of its head. The rabbit attempted to kick and escape at the unexpected touch, but Andy held on to it with a firm grip. Throughout the entire scene, Madge watched, quietly laughing to herself.

"We need to get out of the middle of the street," Madge finally mentioned, as a car swerved to go around them.

"Ok," Andy replied. "Nichole, grab my shirt, and you can hold the rabbit in it, but you have to hold real tight so it does not get loose while I am driving."

Nichole nodded and bent over to pick up his shirt off the truck floor. She spread it across her lap as she folded her legs in front of her. Andy lifted the rabbit away from his bare chest and slowly placed it in Nichole's lap. "Ok, now wrap the shirt around it so it cannot scratch you," Andy instructed. Nichole gathered up the sides of the shirt as Andy kept his hands gripped on the rabbit's legs. Once Nichole had wrapped the rabbit in the shirt, and it had stopped squirming, again he released one finger at a time and slipped his hands out of the shirt. Nichole gripped the sides together with both hands as the rabbit sat in the shirt on her lap. "Its heart is beating so fast!" Nichole exclaimed. "Yeah, it is had a pretty exciting night," Andy answered.

He shifted the truck into drive and drove down the street, back on to his task of finding a place to park for the night. After a while, he found a dark secluded street that appeared to get little traffic, and, by now, it was already the middle of the night. He slowed the truck and pulled off to the side of the road.

Nichole kept her attention fixed on the rabbit burrowed in the shirt in her lap. Its breathing and heartbeat had finally slowed down to normal. She slowly pulled the sides of the shirt apart and peeked inside. The rabbit's ears lay down across its back but it stayed still. Nichole slowly bent one finger down and stroked its back so lightly she was not even sure if she had actually touched it. When the rabbit did not attempt to escape, she stroked it again, this time tracing the outline of a white patch that ran down its back. "It is so soft, Daddy!" She whispered. Andy turned and looked at her, "Yeah. Look! It is finally calmed down. What are you going to call it?" He asked.

Nichole looked up at him, wrinkled her forehead and then looked up to the ceiling of the truck. "I do not know...is it a boy or a girl?" She looked down at the rabbit, trying to decide if it looked more like a girl or a boy.

"Let me check," Andy answered and reached into the shirt gripping the rabbit from behind and reaching his fingers around it to hold its legs from kicking again. He turned the rabbit over and announced, "It is a girl!" He then gently placed the rabbit back in the shirt on Nichole's lap and helped her hold the sides closed until the rabbit sat calmly.

"A girl!" Nichole repeated and started down at her new pet. "What is your name, little bunny?" She asked quietly.

"I am sure you will think of a perfect name," Madge chimed in as she pulled out the blankets from behind the seat and reached to spread them across their laps. "But now we need to get some sleep before it is daylight."

Nichole nodded and stayed in a seated position with her legs crossed in front of her, and the shirt wrapped rabbit falling into an exhausted sleep in her lap. She leaned her head on her mom's shoulder and drifted to sleep with her arms wrapped around her new pet.

CHAPTER 11

Nichole woke with a start before either of her parents. She reached for her new rabbit, but it was gone! She jolted forward and began looking all around her. Her sudden movements woke both of her parents.

"Whoa! What is going on?" Andy cried out startled by the sudden disturbance to his sleep.

"Where is my bunny?" Nichole cried.

Madge looked around them, and there on the floor curled up in the corner of the blanket was the sleeping rabbit.

"There she is!" Nichole exclaimed and reached down to pet the rabbit. The touch woke the sleeping rabbit, and it jumped away. "She is still scared," Nichole told her dad.

"Well, it is going to take a while for her to get used to you," Andy answered. "She was probably someone's pet before she got loose."

"Do you think they miss her?" Nichole wondered.

"Well, she may have been loose for quite a while; she is a bit of a mess." Madge pointed out. For the first time, Nichole noticed the clumps of dirt and burrs stuck to patches of her rabbit's fur.

"She needs a bath and a leash so she does not run away," Nichole told her mom.

"Where are we going to get a leash for a rabbit?" Madge asked.

"I know!" Nichole perked up. "I can make one. We can go dumpster diving one more time, and I can find strings to make her a leash."

"Are you sure you want to do that?" Andy asked, remembering the last time someone had chased them away, and Nichole had been nearly inconsolable.

"Just until we get some string to make a leash, not all day," Nichole explained.

"Ok, if you are sure that you are okay with that," Madge double-checked.

Nichole nodded and bent forward watching her bunny sniffing the trash on the floor.

"Ok, let's go then." Andy slipped the keys into the ignition and turned on the truck. He made a u-turn and they left the cul-de-sac. He drove them to one of the familiar neighborhoods where they used to dumpster dive where no one had ever bothered them. While Andy and Madge worked to get a load of paper for recycling from the trash, Nichole leaned over the sides looking for thrown away shoes with the laces or anything else with string.

After a few dumpsters, Nichole had collected over a dozen pieces of string but insisted that she needed more so that she could braid them together. In one dumpster, she found an old shoe, and when she pulled it out, a square object fell out of the dumpster with it. Nichole was never one to leave trash on the ground and when she climbed down to throw it back in, she noticed that it was a tear off the page daily calendar with a few months' worth of pages left, and each page featured a baby name and its meaning.

Nichole pulled the calendar close and flipped the pages. Every single page contained a name and its meaning. There were boy names and girl names. After removing the laces, she tossed a worn shoe back in the dumpster and ran to show the daily calendar to her mom. "Look what I found!" Nichole waved the calendar over her head. Madge tossed a pile of newspaper in the back of the truck and turned to see what Nichole had found. "Look! It has names!" Nichole announced. "Okay," Madge replied confused. "I can find a name for my new bunny in here," Nichole explained. "Oh! That is wonderful." Madge cheered her daughter's victory.

"Check this out!" Nichole and Madge turned to see Andy holding up a giant blue tarp.

"What is it?" Madge walked closer to get a better look.

"It is a car tarp!" Andy tugged the sides open to show how large it was. "If we find a better place to park at night, we can put this over the truck and sleep in the back."

"Are you sure it will fit over the truck?" Madge asked.

Andy dragged the tarp alongside the truck and spread it out to show that it was almost exactly the length of their truck. "It is perfect!" Andy grinned and folded up the tarp and lifted it into the bed of the truck.

Madge reached in the cab of the truck, pulled out bundles of blankets that she had been collecting from the dumpsters since the beginning, and tucked them under the tarp in the back. "That will make a nice bed if we can find a decent place to park," Madge agreed.

Nichole slipped in the truck under her mother's arm as she was pulling out the blankets to make sure that her bunny was not near the door. Seeing her sniffing something on the other side of the truck, she climbed inside as fast as she could. Once she was inside, she shut the door behind her. A few minutes later, Madge and Andy returned to their doors. Nichole cautioned them to not let her bunny out, and they both opened their doors just enough to slip their bodies through and slammed their doors closed behind them. The bunny darted back and forth at the sudden action but Andy and Madge closed their doors before she could make an escape.

"You better make her a leash soon so we do not have to be afraid to open our doors," Madge warned.

"I will. I have enough string now. We do not have to dumpster dive anymore. Is that okay?" Nichole asked.

"Of course, it is," Madge answered, not wanting to have to go through another dumpster.

"Well, at least we have got a decent load to turn in today," Andy answered.

While they drove to the recycling center, Nichole tied the strings together into three long ropes and then began braiding them together. Once the strings were all braided together, Nichole reached down and wrapped it around her bunny's neck making sure it would not be too tight, but small enough that she could not slip out.

"Let me show you a trick," Madge reached for the braided leash. Nichole handed it to her, and Madge re-tied the loop to go around the rabbit's neck a little looser. She reached down, slipped the loop over the rabbit's head, pulled it across its back, and then around the rabbit's chest just behind its front legs. Madge fashioned a second knot to hold this loop in place.

"Now she will not run away!" Nichole grinned at her mom's cleverness.

While they were working on the leash, Andy had been unloading their recycling from the bed of the truck and had wound back around for the empty truck weight. When Andy parked to go to the cashier to collect their money, Nichole requested to go with him and test out her new leash.

Andy examined the leash Madge and Nichole had created and consented for her to join him in line. In the line, a woman was standing in front of them and she noticed their rabbit. "Well, isn't that a cute bunny!" She smiled to Nichole, revealingly a mouth of mostly missing teeth. The stranger's attention brought out Nichole's shyness, and she leaned against her dad but remembered to say, "Thank you." Andy rubbed Nichole's shoulder and struck up a conversation with the woman.

She was homeless too, in her car, and they talked for a while about the challenge of finding a place to park and sleep at night. The woman mentioned a field that she had been parking at that was good. She explained that there were a few other homeless families there and everyone left each other alone. Andy thanked her for the tip, and they each approached the two cashier windows to collect their money and went their separate ways. Nichole gripped Andy's hand with one hand and her bunny's leash with the other. Most of the time, the bunny hopped obediently beside them. It only needed a gentle tug on the leash from Nichole when it started to hop off in the wrong direction.

Back at the truck, Nichole scooped up her bunny holding onto its feet like her dad had shown her to make sure it did not kick her. Andy helped lift her into the truck since her hands were busy holding onto the rabbit. He plopped her in the middle seat and slid in next to her.

As he drove to make a drug pick up, Andy told Madge about the woman in the line and the area that they may be able to park and sleep at night.

"We should go check it out," Madge suggested.

"Yeah, we will after we get a fix," Andy answered.

He drove to the drug dealer's house, made a fast exchange, and returned to the truck. He drove them to a park where Nichole could play with her new rabbit while they got high.

At the park, Nichole carried her bunny to a grassy area where it feasted on tall grass. Nichole sat beside her and flipped through the pages of the calendar of daily baby names. Each time she found a girl's name, she would say it aloud and watch to see if the bunny had any reaction. "Ashley...Mary...Stephanie...Emily..." Each time the bunny just kept munching on the grass. "Bethany...Carolina...Elizabeth...Chloe."

Suddenly the bunny stopped eating and looked up at her. Nichole gasped and repeated, "Chloe." The bunny wriggled her nose in the air and then resumed eating the grass. "I guess that means you like 'Chloe' for your name" Nichole tore off the page from the calendar and stuffed it in her pocket before tossing the rest of the name calendar in the nearest trashcan. She looked back to the page on the calendar. "It says the name Chloe is Greek and means 'green shoot.' Well, I guess you like to eat green shoots of grass so that works." Nichole giggled.

While Nichole stretched out the length of Chloe's leash, she realized that she could tie the end of the leash to the pole at the swings. This way she could swing while she watched her bunny munching on the grass and hopping around.

A few other kids were playing on the jungle gym and slides, and, when they noticed that Nichole had a bunny, they ran over to say 'Hi'.

Nichole slipped off the swings as they approached and grabbed the leash. Her dad had taught her to be cautious of everybody.

A little boy with dark brown hair and brown eyes approached first. "Is that your bunny?" He asked.

Nichole sat close to her bunny with the leash wrapped so that the bunny remained close by her side. "Yeah, my daddy got her for me. Her name is Chloe." Nichole answered the boy.

"Can I pet her?" He asked.

"Um, ok. Just be gentle because she gets scared." Nichole warned him.

The boy bent down on his hands and knees and crawled close until he could touch Chloe. With one hand then he rubbed the top of her head. "She is so soft." Nichole agreed.

"Can my sister pet her too?" he asked. Nichole looked over at the sister who was a little bit older than the boy was but was a bit shyer. She had the same dark hair and dark eyes, but her hair was long and split into two flowing pigtails.

"Yeah, she can pet her, but she just needs to be gentle."

"Come here, Anna!" The boy called out. "The bunny is nice. Come feel how soft it is." Slowly the girl approached, and as she got closer, she bent down to her hands and knees and crawled until she was sitting beside her brother in the grass. "You can pet her, but just be gentle," her brother explained. The girl reached out and ran her fingers down Chloe's back. "She is soft," she whispered. The three kids chatted for a while and then crawled around the grass following Chloe as she found fresh patches of grass to nibble on.

After a while, the brother and sister's mom called them telling them that it was time to go. As they said their goodbyes to Chloe and

Nichole the boy called out, "You are so lucky you get to have a bunny. My mom will not let as have any pets at our house."

Nichole waved goodbye, pondering his words that he thought she was lucky for having a pet. But he had a house. Nichole climbed to her feet and wiped her hands on her jeans to shake off the dirt and grass from crawling on the ground and then she returned to her parents in the truck.

Andy was reading a newspaper, and Madge had been watching Nichole from her window. Nichole picked up Chloe and lifted her into the truck, where she announced the name she had settled on for her bunny and how, in fact, Chloe had chosen the name herself. Madge asked her about the kids she had been talking to, and Nichole shared about how they liked Chloe and how the boy wished that he had his own pet, even though he already has a house to sleep in.

CHAPTER 12

Madge tucked away their foil, straws, and lighter in the truck's glove box, and Nichole settled in the middle seat between her parents and buckled her seat belt. Nichole patted her dad's hand as it rested on the steering wheel. "Where are we going to sleep tonight, Daddy?" She asked.

"Oh, that is right!" He lifted his head and looked at Nichole. "We need to check out the field that lady was telling us about."

Andy shifted the truck into drive and pulled away from the park. He took the freeway until he spotted the c\City's water tower. "It is over there," Andy pointed and took the next exit off the freeway. They had to weave up and down streets until they reached the street that led to the City's water tower. There was a gate around most of the field under the tower but there was an opening just large enough to fit their truck. Before pulling into the field, Andy pulled the truck to the side of the road and got out to check it out on foot.

Andy walked through the opening in the gate and scanned the area. In the corner, along one side of the fence, a few tents were set up. If anybody was in them, they made no effort to come out to meet him.

Andy walked in a full circle. He liked how the fence provided privacy without trapping them in. After his inspection, he strolled back to the truck and climbed in.

"It looks pretty good," Andy shared with Madge and Nichole. "We can use the tarp cover we found and sleep in the back like a real bed again."

"Are you sure we will not be disturbed?" Madge asked.

"Yeah, there are some tents, but they are all spread apart like everyone leaves each other alone," Andy reassured her. "In fact, if there is any trouble, we would have a lot more lookouts."

Madge nodded that she was willing to sleep there for the night.

Since the sun was almost setting, they decided to start setting up for the night right away. Andy shifted the truck into drive and drove onto the field through the narrow opening. He rolled the truck slowly over the dry cracked dirt that covered the entire field, except for the occasional weed that managed to peek its head through. Andy drove the truck to the side of the field where nobody else was and parked.

Andy jumped out of the driver's seat, pulled the large tarp from the bed of the truck and began shaking it out. He spread it out on the ground behind the truck and tossed it from side to side and flipped in over until he had found the front and back for it to fit over the truck.

Meanwhile, Madge was arranging their ever-growing collection of blankets and sleeping bags in the bed of the truck. Every single time they had gone dumpster diving she had gathered a new blanket that someone else had thrown out. Now she was able to spread them out and layer them until the bed of the truck was several layers deep in blankets. The majority of them she spread out for cushion, and a few would cover them for warmth. Madge sorted through all of them and checked for soils and stains. She selected the two cleanest blankets to serve as the sheets.

Andy peered in the back of the truck to see the bed that Madge had made. "That actually looks comfortable," he acknowledged.

"Yeah," Madge answered, "we may actually get a good night's sleep for once."

Andy motioned for Madge to join him behind the truck where he had the tarp spread out. "Grab that side," he motioned to the top corner of the tarp, "so we can pull it straight over the top."

Madge bent down and grabbed the top corner and together they lifted the tarp high and walked along both sides of the truck until they had pulled their sides over the cab. Andy bent down, tied the string in his corner of the tarp to the front bumper, and then ran around to do their same to Madge's side. He continued around to the back, securing all four corners so that it would blow off in the middle of the night.

Inside the truck, Nichole looked up when everything around her turned blue as her parents pulled the giant tarp up over all of the windows. She turned in her seat where she had been petting her rabbit and saw the bed in the back that her mom had made. It looked like the grandest bed Nichole had seen in a long time.

Before going to bed, Andy and Madge ducked under the tarp and slipped back in their seats. "Do you want to check out the new bed?" Madge asked. Nichole did, but she also knew that her parents needed their hit for the night before going to bed. Nichole nodded and asked if she could take Chloe on the bed. Madge looked down at the rabbit, "Just for now." Madge opened up the glove box and pulled the foil squares and short straws out. "When we all come to bed, she will need to come back in here, or she may accidentally jump out of the back of the truck during the night."

Nichole agreed and then lifted Chloe through the back window and set her gently on the bed, as Nichole slipped through the window behind her. Nichole looked around the bed her mom had made and saw that she had rolled the blanket at the top in a log shape to serve as a pillow. She peeked her head back in through the window as Andy and Madge were arranging the shiny black balls of heroin on their squares of foil. "Mommy, can you hand me my teddy bear?" Nichole asked. Madge looked over her shoulder to see Nichole's face peeking out the window, and then she looked around to find the teddy bear. Finally, after tossing some papers and wrappers around on the floor, she revealed the stuffed animal and handed it to Nichole through the window. Nichole grabbed the bear and laid it on its back next to the blanket log so she would be able to use it as her pillow by resting her head on its fuzzy stomach.

Nichole turned around to play with Chloe and caught her sniffing the sides of the truck sitting on the mounts of blankets. Nichole saw how easily she could jump over the side, crawled over, and gathered the rabbit in her arms. "You need to be careful, Chloe. If you jump over the sides, you could get hurt." Nichole continued talking to her rabbit while Madge finished her hit and Andy was just starting another.

Madge cracked her door open, slipped out, and quietly closed it behind her. Pressed against the side of the truck under the tarp, Madge scooted her way along the side until she got to the back tire and used it as a step to climb up into the bed with Nichole and Chloe. The tarp was lower at the far end of the truck and higher where it had to cover the cab, so once Madge crawled to the top of the bed, where she could sit up comfortably.

Nichole crawled close to her mom, with Chloe tucked in her arm, and they sat together. Nichole sat Chloe in her lap, and, while Nichole played with her rabbit, Madge ran her fingers through her daughter's head, trying to remove the tangled clumps. Nichole turned and glanced in the cab and saw her dad's head dipping forward and bobbing up and down with his eyes half closed. Her mom called this "nodding." And while her dad did this every single time he got high, she never saw her mom "nodding.." Madge had explained to her that she only took enough heroin keep from getting sick, but her dad liked to get completely high.

Nichole turned back around and saw that her mom was pulling back a layer of the blankets to slip in bed. "Ok, go ahead and put Chloe back inside and we will get ready for bed." Madge pushed and prodded on the blanket log to make it cradle her head comfortably. Nichole picked up her rabbit and slipped her in through the window setting her gently on the seat. Chloe jumped off the seat, onto the floor, and burrowed a tunnel under the papers and trash to make she own bed for the night. Andy remained in the cab bobbing his head with a blank expression on his face. Nichole crawled under the blankets beside her mom and rested her head on her teddy bear.

Nichole laid there staring at the blue tarp ceiling for a few minutes. Then she turned on her side to look at her mom. "Mommy, can we do a bedtime story tonight?" Madge turned on her side to face Nichole, "Of course, Baby! What story do you want?"

"I want a 'me' story!" Nichole grinned, and before Madge could think of a way to begin the story, Nichole began, "Once upon a time, there was a girl named Nichole, and she lived in a castle and had lots of different animals that she rescued."

Nichole stopped and looked at Madge waiting for her to continue the story. "Um," Madge thought for a moment, "One day Nichole was going for a walk in the forest next to her castle, and as she was walking she saw something."

"What was it?" Nichole asked.

"What do you want it to be?" Madge replied.

"It was a..." Nichole clenched her eyes shut and scrunched up her face as she thought. Her eyes popped open. "It was a time machine!" Nichole announced.

"It was?" Madge asked, encouraging Nichole to continue the story.

Nichole continued the story, "Yes, it was a time machine, and so Nichole decided to look inside. There were buttons and lights everywhere, and, when Nichole got inside, the door accidentally closed, and the lights started flashing. When Nichole tried to open the door, she accidentally moved a lever that slipped up to a label that read 'Caveman Days'."

Madge laughed at her daughter's clever imagination. "Caveman times?"

"Yeah," Nichole giggled and continued, "So Nichole was stuck inside the time machine, and it was shaking, and the lights were flashing, but then the lights just stopped, and the door pops open a little bit."

Nichole paused and grinned, "Okay, your turn, Mommy."

"Okay," Madge began, "Nichole pushed the door all the way open and stepped outside. She looked all around her, and there were trees everywhere, like a forest. She thought about going exploring in the forest, but she heard a sound on the other side of the time machine, so she went to go see what it was."

When Madge stopped, Nichole took that as her cue to pick up the story. "Nichole walked all around the time machine. And at first, she did not see anything, but then she noticed something hiding behind a big rock."

Madge continued where Nichole left off, "So Nichole called out 'Hello! Who is there?' and the hidden figure ducked down further behind the rock. Nichole kept talking, saying that she was friendly and would not hurt them as she crept closer to the rock. Finally, a head peeked around the rock, and it was a little boy with dark, wild curly hair. Nichole smiled, 'Hi! My name is Nichole. What is your name?' The boy waited a few seconds before answering, 'My name is...'"

Madge trailed off to let Nichole choose the name for the young 'cave boy' she had found.

"He told her, 'My name is George,' Nichole continued the story. "Nichole talked to George for a long time and told him about the time machine, how she came from a different time, and that she had a wonderful castle with lots of animals and friends. However, the boy looked sad. 'Why are you sad?' Nichole asked. The cave boy told Nichole about how his mom and dad had died during a dinosaur hunt, and now he had to live with his mean aunt. George told Nichole that his aunt had hit him and stuff and that he had run away a few days ago, and she did not even notice."

Madge furrowed her eyebrows, "That is very sad, Nichole."

Nichole nodded and tried to explain herself, "I want him to go home with Nichole in the time machine, so he has to have a reason to leave."

"Ok," Madge nodded and allowed Nichole to bring the happy ending to her story.

Nichole continued her story, "So Nichole asked George if he would like to go home with her where no one will ever hurt him, and then he can have fun with all of her animals and she will take care of him. So together then went into the time machine and Nichole found the lever she had moved before and pulled it back to where it had been when she found it. It shakes and the lights flashed again. This time, the little cave boy was scared, but Nichole sat with him and let him know that it would be okay. When the machine stopped, the door opened, and Nichole took him to her home, introduced him to her family and friends, and gave him his own room in her castle and showed him all of her animals. Then he lived happily ever after, and Nichole kept going on more adventures to help people. The end!"

"Wow!" Madge yawned, "That was quite a bedtime story. Are you ready to go to sleep now?"

Nichole nodded and snuggled down further into the blankets. At the same time, Andy climbed out of the cab of the truck and into the bed.

Nichole was safe and warm between her parents, and she drifted off to sleep.

Once she saw that Nichole was asleep, Madge asked Andy, "How much did you use? Are we going to have enough to last until we get some more money?"

Andy tilted his head to face Madge over the top of Nichole's head. "I finished it." Before Madge could get upset, he tried to justify. "I have an idea on how we will get some money tomorrow."

It did not work, and Madge did get upset. In a stern whisper as to not wake Nichole, she chided him, "What is your idea now? If it does not work, we are going to be sick and unable to take care of Nichole!"

"Relax!" Andy turned his head forward to stare at their tarp ceiling, "We will just make a 'Will Work For Food' sign and ask people for help."

"Maybe you are!" Madge shook her head. "I am not going to sit outside begging."

Andy did not bother to reply and just closed his eyes until he drifted to sleep. Madge rolled her eyes and stroked Nichole's hair until she finally fell asleep too.

CHAPTER 13

By morning, all three were still sleeping. The sun was already up, but the cover of the blue tarp hid how bright it was. During the night, a couple of other cars had pulled in and parked on the field too. When one of the cars turned on and drove out the opening in the fence, the sound woke Madge. She sat up in their bed and stretched, with her arms reaching out as far as they could. She let out a long yawn and looked around her. Andy and Nichole were still asleep, so she climbed out of the truck bed and slipped under the tarp. It was then that she realized out late they had slept. This was the first night that they all had a restful night's sleep.

Across the field, Madge saw other people gathering up their belongings and hiding them in their tent before they went out for the day. Madge walked around the truck to stand on the side where nobody was to find a private place to use the restroom. When she finished, Andy had started to stir and wake up. Madge looked under the tarp and saw him rubbing his eyes and stretching. "We have got to get going soon," Madge whispered to him. He turned his head to look at her, nodded, and had another stretch. "I need to go to the bathroom first." He placed his hands on the side of the truck while Madge slipped out from under the tarp, and Andy lifted his body over the side of the truck and followed under the tarp.

Madge pointed to where she had gone. "There is a spot where no one can see you," she pointed. Andy walked over to the hidden spot, relieved himself and returned to the truck as soon as he had finished.

Andy walked around the truck, untying the strings that held the tarp in place. Once he had loosened all of the knots, Madge helped him lift the tarp off the truck. Once it was lying on the dirt behind the truck, Madge left him to fold it up while she woke Nichole and put the blankets away. Stepping on the rear bumper, she climbed up and crawled to where Nichole had burrowed further down in the blankets. She had buried herself in the blankets as her parents removed the tarp since the sunlight was now shining in. Madge nudged her shoulders until Nichole's eyes fluttered open. "Good morning," Madge lifted Nichole in her lap. Nichole yawned and attempted to crawl back under the blankets. "Nope, we will have to get going." Madge tugged Nichole back. "Why don't you go get in the front and check on Chloe?"

Nichole suddenly became more alert, and, without another word, she turned and crawled through the rear window from the bed into the cab and picked up her rabbit from off the floor and began stroking her fur.

In the back, Madge crawled to the foot of the bed and rolled all of the blankets at once in a giant log that rested on top of the pillow log at the top of the truck bed.

Andy picked up the tarp he had folded and tossed it in the truck. Madge pulled it over the blankets and undid one fold to make it cover all of their blankets. With their tasks completed, they both got into the truck.

Nichole watched as her parents climbed into the truck on either side of her. She held Chloe firmly in her lap so that she would not run out when the doors opened. Once everyone was inside, Nichole turned to her dad. "What are we going to do today, Daddy?"

Andy rubbed the rabbit before talking. "We are going to make a sign and ask if people will help us."

Nichole thought about this for a moment. "Will they really help us?"

"Some people will," Andy answered, as he started the truck and drove off the field through the opening in the fence.

Madge shook her head. "I already told you, I am not begging."

"That is fine." Andy shrugged.

"I will help you, Daddy!" Nichole offered.

"Thank you." Andy glanced over Nichole's head at Madge and grinned. Madge turned her head to look out the window and ignore him.

Andy drove to a grocery store just a few miles from where they used to live. He pulled behind the store in the alley and parked beside a pile of produce boxes. The employees flattened each box and left them in a stack for pick up. Andy got out of the truck and picked up one box. He flipped it over and grabbed one of the flaps. He swiftly tore the flap off, tossed the box back onto the pile and got back in the truck. "Here's our sign!" Andy dropped the piece of cardboard onto Nichole's lap.

"What do we do with it?" Nichole turned it over in her hands.

"We need to write a message on it!" He fumbled through papers on the dash until he found a pen. Taking the sign from Nichole, he scribbled in large letters "WILL WORK FOR FOOD." He then handed the sign and the pen back to Nichole. "Now made the letters bigger and darker so people can see them."

Nichole took the pen and scribbled up and down over her father's writing as he had instructed. After a few minutes, she lifted the sign to show Andy.

He took the sign from Nichole and inspected it. "Perfect! Are you ready to get to work?"

Nichole nodded, and Andy drove the truck around to the front of the grocery store and parked in the back of the parking lot. Andy stepped out his door, and Nichole followed. Madge stayed in the car and found the book she had found in a dumpster. She turned to the first page and read while Andy and Nichole went out to beg for money.

Hand in hand, Andy and Nichole walked to the front of the grocery store. They found a spot on the short brick wall near the parking lot exit. They sat where they could meet the traffic of people driving through the parking lot and those walking in the store. Andy lifted Nichole onto his lap and together they held the sign. Several cars drove by, and people walked in and out of the store without looking at them. "Daddy, why does our sign just say that we need food? We mostly need money."

"People will be able to tell that we need money, and by offering to work is the most respectful way to ask for help. And if someone has some work that I can do, then I will do it."

Nichole thought about this for a moment and then nodded before placing her hands on the sides of the sign next to her dad's hands. They had not received any money yet, but Nichole decided that she liked this a lot better than stinky dumpster diving.

A line of cars stretched in front of them as people were waiting to pull out onto the road. One car rolled down their window and waved their hand. Andy nudged Nichole, "Look, someone has something for us!" Nichole looked up and saw the car, "Can I go get it, Daddy?" Andy looked from side to side, "Make sure no cars are coming from the other way, and you can go get it." Nichole slid off her dad's lap and looked both ways before taking the few steps to the car's window. The woman driving the car smiled and handed Nichole a dollar. "Thank you!" Nichole took the dollar turned checked for cars and ran back her dad's lap. "Look, Daddy! She gave us a dollar!" "Good job! You are doing great."

Nichole grinned and started smiling at every single car that passed by. By lunchtime, they had received a few more dollars and several handfuls of change. "I am hungry." Nichole squirmed in her father's lap. "Let's go get some food," Andy suggested. Andy checked his pockets for the few food stamps they had left. "How about we get some cup of noodles?" Nichole agreed, and together they walked into the grocery store and found the pasta aisle. Andy picked a chicken cup for himself, a beef cup for Madge, and Nichole chose a shrimp cup for herself.

At the checkout line, Andy gave Nichole a food stamp dollar and instructed her to buy her cup separately so that they could get the coin change back. The cashier rang up the one cup, and Nichole handed her the food stamp. The cashier looked at the little girl and then over to her dad. "She likes to be a big girl and buy her own food," Andy explained, while the cashier counted out Nichole's change and handed it to her. The cashier made no comment while she rang up Andy's purchase and gave him the appropriate change for his. Andy and Nichole walked out of the grocery store hand in hand. They walked across the parking lot to the truck where Madge was waiting and showed her what they had bought and how much money they had made with their sign.

"How are we going to cook these?" Madge took the cup of noodles that Andy handed to her.

Andy pointed across the street. "There is a microwave in that 7-Eleven."

Andy stepped back out of the truck, Nichole followed behind him, and Madge opened her door to climb out and join them. Together all three walked on the crosswalk to the 7-Eleven on the corner.

"Hide your cup of noodles in your jacket." Andy demonstrated by slipping his cup inside his jacket and tucking it under his arm. "They probably do not want people bringing in their own food."

"Why did not we buy our noodles here?" Nichole looked up at her dad as she attempted to hide her cup under her jacket, even though the cup took up a lot more space in her jacket than it did in her father's jacket.

"This 7-Evelen doesn't like to take food stamps," Andy explained to her.

Andy opened the door to the small store, and Madge and Nichole walked in ahead of them. Madge guided Nichole to follow her as they walked around a few aisles before arriving at the microwave. Andy pretended to be browsing one of the shelves while Madge filled all three cups with water from the drinking fountain and then put them in the microwave. While their cups cooked, they walked around. When the timer dinged on the microwave, Madge retrieved their cups and slipped a handful of plastic forks from the rack. Andy bought a pack of cigarettes and a king size Reese's candy bar to keep the cashier's attention while Madge and Nichole retrieved their cups and walked out the store. When Andy came out, Madge handed him his cup, and they let Nichole hold the forks and the Reese's so that she would not accidentally spill the hot water on herself as they walked back across the street to their truck.

Inside the truck, they ate their noodles and sipped the broth. Once they had all finished their cups, Andy opened the Reese's, they each ate one Reese's cup, and Andy saved the fourth cup for later.

Over the next several days, Andy and Nichole continued working with their sign and getting just enough to get them food and to satisfy Andy and Madge's addiction.

Nichole grew to enjoy working with the sign with her dad because so many people were friendly. One day a man even gave them a twenty-dollar bill! Nichole was so excited she kept asked her dad to take it out of his pocket so she could see it. They say they collected more money than they ever had before. "Maybe we will do something special today," Andy suggested.

Just before they were going to stop for the day, a woman pulled up her car next to them. She stepped out and walked around to the back to open her trunk. Inside the trunk were bags full of groceries. "Would you like some food?" The woman rummaged through her bags.

"We would greatly appreciate that." Andy stepped forward to accept a bag that she had separated from the rest. The woman looked from Andy down to Nichole and back to Andy. "Well, you know it really sickens me that you have such a young child out here with you doing your dirty work. I would never give you any on my money because I just do not know what you would do with it because, obviously, you are not taking good care of this little girl." Nichole looked up at the woman with tears collecting on her eyelids. She tried not to blink because she knew they would start streaming down her face if she did.

This was a new kind of cruelty that Nichole had never experienced before. On one hand, the woman was being nice by giving them some of her food, but, at the same time, she was belittling and shaming them. Nichole decided that she did not even want to take food from her. "I would rather starve than take food from someone like you!" Nichole screamed, as the tears finally spilled down her cheeks. She then ran across the parking lot to their truck. As far as Nichole understood, an insult to her parents was an insult to her because they looked out for each other. Andy accepted the bag of food from the woman before chasing after Nichole.

The woman watched as father and daughter ran away from her with the food. "Well! Some people are just so ungrateful!" She tossed her head, slammed the trunk closed, and climbed into her car and sped away.

Back at the truck, Nichole was sobbing in her mother's arms, as Madge was trying to understand what happen. When Andy caught up and climbed in the truck, he explained, "Some witch was insulting us and playing like she was so righteous to be giving us food while she told us how worthless we were."

Between sobs, Nichole added, "Why do people pretend to be nice when they are just mean?"

Madge stroked Nichole's hair and kissed her cheek. They say there for several minutes before Nichole's breathless sobs subsided.

Trying to cheer her up, Andy slipped the twenty-dollar bill from his pocket. "Are you going to show your mom what we got today?"

Nichole perked up and took the twenty from his hand. "A man gave us this much money." She held it up for her mom to see.

"Well, that was very nice of him!" Madge lifted Nichole's chin and looked into her eyes. She would give anything to trying to restore her daughter's faith in people.

Nichole handed the bill back to her dad. "Maybe he was nice, but that old lady was not nice. She thinks she is better than us."

"I know, Baby, but you know that is not true; right?"

Nichole shrugged her shoulders.

Andy shoved the twenty back in his pocket. "Maybe we can find something special to do with this money since it is more than we usually get."

Nichole did not respond, so Andy and Madge discussed the possibilities.

CHAPTER 14

Pizza with extra cheese, a new stuffed animal, or a day at the museum. Nichole was not interested in any of the ideas that her parents came up with to cheer her up with the extra money they had received. She just sat in between them in the truck where they still sat parked in the grocery store parking lot and stroked her rabbit. Nichole thought back to the man who had chased them off while they were dumpster diving and then again the woman today who had treated them so worthlessly. At that moment, Nichole decided to trust no one and that if they wanted anything, they would have to find a way to get it without depending on other people.

After an hour of trying to find a way to spend their extra money to comfort Nichole, Andy started up the truck and drove to a more secluded area where they could have their hit for the night before parking at the water tower.

When they pulled to a stop Nichole immediately climbed through the back window to the truck bed with Chloe, lay down, and stared at the sky while her rabbit hopped around her, and even sometimes hopped right across her tummy.

Inside, Andy and Madge pulled out their last bit of heroin. As they were arranging their foil, straws and lighter, Madge got an idea. "Why don't we get a motel room tonight with the extra money?"

Andy nodded, "That is not a bad idea. What do you think, Nichole?" He called out through the window.

"What?" Nichole sat up and slid herself closer to the window.

"Do you want to get a motel room for the night with the money we got?"

Nichole considered for a moment, "Does it have TV?"

Andy laughed, "Of course, it has TV!"

Nichole perked up, "Yeah! Let's stay in a motel room!"

"It also will have a shower!" Madge added. "It is about time we got cleaned up."

"I hope it has a bathtub instead of just a shower," Nichole answered.

"Ok!" Andy announced. "We will finish this hit and go get a motel room. Then you get to have your shower or bath while I go make a pick up since this is the last of our stash. And then you can watch TV until you fall asleep."

Nichole and Madge agreed on his plan. Nichole returned to playing with her rabbit in the back of the truck while her parents finished their last hit, which was not nearly enough to satisfy their increasing addiction, and certainly was not enough to get high.

After a few minutes, they finished their tiny stash and were ready to find a motel room. Andy drove to the nearest gas station to use the pay phone to call his dealer and then he browsed through the yellow pages until he found the cheapest motel he could. It was several miles away but no other motel could come close to their price. While Andy was making his calls, Nichole searched the seats for loose change so that they could get a little bit of gas before going to find their motel.

Andy drove the truck on the freeway several miles before he got off, and they found themselves pulling in a motel with a sign in the front that read "Fire Station Motel." Nichole looked around and could not see any reasons why someone would decide to name this motel after a fire station. Andy parked in front of the office and ran inside to get a room. Nichole looked around at the buildings that stretched in a boxy U shape with a large grassy area in the middle. It even had a swimming pool! The sun had started to set, so nobody was in the pool, but a few people were scurrying around on the field. Andy came out of the office with a key, and then he hopped back into the truck. He drove around until they pulled into a parking space in front of their room.

They piled out of the truck and stood in front of the door while Andy jiggled the key until the door opened. Nichole was holding onto Chloe's leash and guided her rabbit to follow her inside. The room was everything Nichole had hoped for! There were two beds with a table holding a lamp on either side of them. There was a dresser for storing clothes and things. In addition, high up on the wall was a small TV. Nichole ran and jumped onto the bed and bounced up and down and then jumped from one bed to the other while Chloe sniffed around on the floor.

Andy and Madge laughed at Nichole's excitement. Their greatest relief was to see her not thinking about the woman who had insulted them earlier that day. Nichole jumped off the bed and landed on the floor in front of her parents. "Is there a bathtub?" Madge reached out for Nichole's hand. "Let's go check and see!" Together they walked into the bathroom and there was a sink, a toilet, and a pulled shower curtain. Nichole drew the curtain back and squealed when she saw the full bathtub. She turned and hugged her mom and then ran to hug her dad. "Thank you for getting us a room. Our new bed in the truck is nice since we found a good place to park, but a real bed with a TV and a bathtub are way better."

Madge was happy to see her daughter so excited. In Nichole's excitement, she only saw the best in the room, but Madge noticed the cockroaches that ran under the counter when she turned on the bathroom light. There were also stains and burn holes in the blankets and carpet. However, she would not mention any of these things as not to dampen her daughter's mood.

Andy gave the room a quick glance. He felt satisfied by his daughter's reaction. "I am going to go make our pick-up, and then we can finish getting well," he told Madge. Even though they had had a small hit of heroin earlier, it was not the amount they had come to require. Andy's hands were already starting to tremble slightly.

"Can I watch cartoons now, Mommy?" Nichole sat perched on the edge of one of the beds.

"How about you have your bath first and then you can watch cartoons," Madge suggested.

"Okay!" Nichole slid off the edge of the bed and walked into the bathroom.

Madge turned on the faucets and adjusted them until she had gentle warm water flowing in the tub. She pressed the plug over the drain while Nichole slipped out of her tattered clothes. As the water was still filling in the tub, Nichole lifted one bare foot over the side testing the water. Once she decided that it was just right, she climbed into the tub and sat down. Madge knelt beside the tub, grabbed one of the miniature bottles of soap and poured a little in her hands. She rubbed both hands together until the soap lathered, and then reached out and massaged it in Nichole's hair. While Madge washed Nichole's hair, Nichole scooped up handfuls of water and let it run over her arms.

"Ready to rinse?" Madge grabbed an empty plastic cup off the counter and dropped it in the water.

Nichole nodded and clapped both of her hands over her eyes as Madge poured several cups of water over her head.

"All done." Madge picked up Nichole's wet clump of hair and wrung it in her hands to get out all of the soap and water. Nichole looked down in the water which was now filled with bunches of suds. Madge let Nichole play in the water for a few more minutes before grabbing a white towel off the rack and holding it out. Nichole stood up in the water and Madge wrapped the length of the towel around her and lifted her out of the tub. Nichole shivered and clung to the warmth of the towel while Madge retrieved her change of clothes.

Nichole slipped into her cleanest outfit. Madge followed her into the room as Nichole climbed up on the bed and slid under the covers with a pillow propped behind her so she could sit up. Madge reached up on her tiptoes to turn on the TV hanging on the wall and turned the dial until she found cartoons. Nichole sat transfixed as she watched TV for the first time in months.

With Nichole occupied, Madge returned to the bathroom, where she drained the murky water from Nichole's bath and drew a fresh bath for herself. She turned the water much warmer than she had for her daughter, sank in the warm tub, and laid back with her eyes closed, embracing the first chance to relax. Finally, she sat up and used the soap to wash her body. By the time she got out, toweled off and was dressed, she came out of the bathroom to find Nichole fast asleep. Madge smiled and turned the channel to a soap opera before slipping into the bed with her daughter.

While they were bathing and watching TV, Andy had left to go pick up some drugs from his dealer. Before leaving, he walked to the pay phone near the office, which was now closed. Andy called his dealer to let him know what time he would be by to pick up. As soon as he hung up the phone, he pulled his cash out of his pocket to count how much he would be able to purchase. Across the parking lot in the shadows, two young men saw Andy counting his money. As Andy started walking back toward his truck, one of the men emerged from the darkness and approached him.

"Hey! You got a light?" He called out to Andy.

Andy looked around and realized that he was talking to him and, not wanting to slow down he called back. "Nah. Sorry!"

The young man closed the gap between them until he was walking in the same stride alongside Andy. "Are you sure? I just need a quick light."

While the young man was distracting him, his friend circled around behind them until he appeared on the other side of Andy. "Then how about you give us your money instead?"

Andy looked from side to side at both men and told them to leave him alone before he made them regret it. Unfortunately, Andy was not at full strength since he was so desperate for his next hit and both men overpowered him. They shoved him against the wall of the nearest building, punched, and kicked him until his face bled, and then he collapsed to his knees doubled over trying to block their attacks. After beating on him for several minutes, one of them reached into his pocket and took all of his cash. As soon as they had the money, they ran off, leaving Andy bleeding and groaning on the ground. On his hands and knees, Andy crawled back to their room and pounded on the door.

The sound startled Madge, and she jumped out of the bed. "Who is it?"

"It's Andy! Open the door!" Andy coughed and blood dripped out of his mouth as he sat in front of the door.

Madge opened the door and found Andy sitting in a bloody, sobbing mess. "What happened to you?" She cried out.

Andy pulled himself in the room. "Some punks robbed me! They took all of our money, Madge! That was all of it!"

Madge helped Andy onto the second bed and ran to the bathroom to get a wet washcloth to clean up his face. Andy lay on the bed moaning and crying as Madge wiped away the blood. "We cannot get our fix now," he kept stammering repeatedly. A fit of coughing hit him, and he doubled over, clutching his ribs, and then wiped his mouth with a cloth, covering it with blood. They had nearly knocked out one of his remaining teeth.

Once Madge had cleaned his face, she could see that his nose had been broken and one tooth was wiggling, as he cried more from frustration over losing the money that from the beating he had received.

Madge left the room to retrieve some ice from the machine. When she returned, she helped Andy remove his shirt over his head. Bruises had already started to form along his ribs. Madge wrapped a bunch of ice in a washcloth and gave it to Andy to hold against his ribs. He remained laying on the bed curled up on his side, holding the ice pack against his skin. He moaned and cursed until he fell asleep.

When Madge saw that, he had fallen asleep on top of the blankets, she went to the closet and grabbed an extra sheet to lay over him. Madge paced back and forth in the room, anxious over what they were going to do next since she could already feel her stomach rumbling in protest for not getting enough heroin that day. She could only imagine what Andy was experiencing since he was accustomed to a much larger daily hit than she was. At this point, it was difficult to distinguish between his pain from the beating and any withdrawals he may be starting to experience.

Madge climbed back into bed with Nichole, who had only stirred slightly from all of the noise in their room. At this moment, Madge was thankful that her daughter was such a deep sleeper. Madge turned off the lamp beside the bed and lay in the darkness, listening to Nichole breathing and Andy's moans as he slept fitfully. After several hours of lying on the bed, staring into the darkness, Madge finally fell asleep.

CHAPTER 15

Throughout the night, Andy continued to moan in pain. Nightmares ravaged his sleep. He would wake breathless from fear, sit up on the bed, look around the dark motel room, and lay back down to repeat the whole process again a few hours.

Madge did not sleep more than a few minutes all night, as every single sound kept her awake. Andy's cries, sirens screaming by throughout the night, neighbors in the motel fighting. She watched her daughter sleeping beside her and vowed that if she could get clean, she would do everything she could to take care of her.

Just before the sun arose, Andy jolted up on his bed. He had had a dream that he found a stash of heroin in his truck, and then he ran out the door to find it. His bruised ribs throbbed, reminding him that he could not move so fast. At the truck, he grabbed handfuls of trash off the floor and threw it on the ground beside where he knelt and meticulously leafed through every single piece looking for a tiny black ball of heroin. When Madge went outside to check on him, trash surrounded him, and he was digging with his hands under the seats. Madge stood and watched him for a minute before he walked back into the room.

She turned on the TV, looking for a distraction from her craving and Andy's anxious search. While Nichole continued to sleep, Madge sat beside her and used her fingers to get rid of some of the tangles in her daughter's hair.

Andy ran back into the room breathless, with sweat streaming down his face. His nose had started to bleed again. He ran into the bathroom and doubled over the toilet. Madge could hear him panting for breath as he vomited repeatedly. Just as she had suspected their withdrawals were beginning. Madge was not surprised that Andy would get them sooner and stronger than she would. He had always used so much more than she had. He even sometimes used multiple times per day.

Andy's stomach clenched violently as he continued to throw up into the toilet. Even on a nearly empty stomach, the vomit would not stop, even when all that would come up was bright yellow burning bile. His sides screamed out in agony where he had been kicked the night before. Gradually he started to hurt more and more and not just in places where he had been hit. He screamed out as the feeling of knives pierced up and down his back. He thought that his feet and hands would burst from the pain. Worst of all was the continuing spasms in his stomach that left him heaving with nothing to come out. The heaving spasms came so quickly one right after another so that he could not even catch his breath, and he collapsed on the floor gasping for air. As he lay there, his legs began jolting violently, first one and then the other. "Make it stop!" He screamed in terror.

All of the noise finally woke Nichole, and she walked to where her mom stood to watch her dad. Nichole had never seen her dad so terrified before in her life. The smell of vomit filled the room and Nichole wondered if it was going to make her vomit as well. Madge did not have to wonder because the combination of watching Andy and her own withdrawals beginning, she found a trash can and emptied her stomach into it. She was relieved that her withdrawals were not as severe as Andy's were.

"Oh, that stinks!" Andy cried out, as he pulled himself back up into a seated position and flushed the toilet before heaving over it again, though nothing came out anymore. Sweat dripped off every part of him, but it felt like stinging ice against his skin. His teeth chattered as he cried out, "s...s...so cold."

Nichole ran to his bed and tugged the blanket off the top. She dragged it into the bathroom and lifted it over her dad's shoulders. He clung to the blanket and fell back over on his side sobbing. His mind swam with anxiety. He imagined himself dying on the floor of a cheap motel bathroom with his daughter watching. The reminders came flooding into his mind of what a screw up he was. Everything he had ever done to disappoint people. He decided that he was as likely as not just better off dead, but before he could complete that thought, his craving reminded him that just a small hit of heroin would make this all go away. Andy rolled on the bathroom floor moaning helplessly because he could not think of a single way for them to get even the tiniest hit.

Meanwhile, Madge only had to relieve her stomach a couple of times before she was able to sit still and catch her breath. Nichole had removed the blanket from their bed and dragged it over to where Madge sat. "Thank you, Baby."

Nichole pulled Madge's hair out of her face and secured it with a piece of string she had found on the floor.

While her parents battled their withdrawals, Nichole pulled a chair under the TV and stood on top of it, balancing each of her feet on the armrests so that she could reach the knob. She turned the knob one click, and the TV blinked to life. She watched the pictures on the screen and kept turning the knob until it stopped on The Power Rangers. Nichole looked over her shoulder before jumping from her perch on the chair and landing with a bounce on the bed. The sounds of the Power Rangers defeating another villain helped to drown out the cries of her father.

Her mother had collected herself somewhat and scooted over so she could sit propped against the side of the bed. Nichole watched show after show as her parents remained sick. Andy's vomiting had slowed down and then he crawled his way into the room. "We need to get a fix." He pulled himself into a seated position beside Madge. "How? We do not have any money!" She reminded him. Andy shook his head and dropped it in his hands. "No, no, no." Madge watched him as he schemed for an answer. His head jerked up. "A clinic!"

"A what?" Madge looked at him with confusion.

"There is a methadone clinic we can go to!"

Methadone was a prescribed alternative to heroin. It did not give the same high, but it would help relieve their withdrawals and cravings.

With a glimmer of hope from his new idea, he then tried to stand up, but the movement caused his stomach to lurch again, so he scampered back in the bathroom. Madge pulled herself up until she was sitting on top of the bed. "Ok, Baby. We need to get everything loaded back into the truck so we can go to the clinic and then get well.

Nichole nodded and climbed off the bed. She retrieved her shoes from under the bed and tied the laces in a bow. Nichole scanned around the room, then picked up a paper bag off the floor, and then scooped her parents' lighters and cigarettes in the bag. She looked around the room and then gathered her bunny in her arms and walked out to the truck.

The doors were locked, so Nichole climbed into the bed of the truck and wiggled the back window open. She dropped the bag inside, gently set Chloe on the seat, and then crawled in the window. From her seat, Nichole reached across both sides and pulled up the locks for both doors.

As she was unlocking her father's door, she looked out the window, and then she saw her mom helping her dad walk from the room to the truck.

He had a plastic bag in his hands that he held close to his face as he continued to seize over with stomach cramps. As they approached, Nichole opened her dad's door so that he could climb inside more easily. Once he was in his seat Nichole reached over him to pull his seatbelt around him, but he pushed her away. "I can't have that across my stomach right now." Nichole nodded and leaned back in her seat. As her mom approached the passenger door, Nichole reached over and held it open for her.

Madge had filled her arms with the motel towels, knowing that they would need something to keep them from being covered in vomit as they drove to the clinic. Once they were all inside, Andy fumbled to find the keys, and, after a brief panic, he discovered them in his pocket. He turned the key in the ignition and then squinted over the steering wheel. After several minutes of staring ahead, Andy pulled the gear into drive and let the truck roll forward. The tires rolled over the trash that he had thrown out of the truck earlier that morning, and then he slowly pulled out of the parking lot and onto the main road.

Andy drove the truck slowly in the far right lane in hopes of not blocking traffic and drawing attention to themselves. He kept a bag on his lap and continued to dry heave over it as he drove. Madge also had a bag, but she was not nearly as sick as Andy was. Nichole helped pay attention to the road, and, when they would stop at a red light, Andy would bend forward and hang his head down as low as he could behind the steering wheel. When the light turned green, Nichole tapped his arm and signal that it was okay to go.

It took them over an hour to reach the clinic. They had to make frequent stops, as his nausea would stop Andy from driving or his leg would start twitching again. At a few points, Nichole placed her hands on the steering wheel to help her dad hold it straight and steady. At one point, Andy had to pull over, jerked the ashtray out of the car, and banged it on the outside of his door to get rid of the smell of the ashes. Everything made him feel ill, especially the smell of cigarettes, which was something he usually enjoyed so much.

At last, they pulled in the parking lot for the clinic. "What do we do? Do we just walk in, and they gave it to us?" Madge asked.

"They will want to make sure we are addicts, and they will set us up on a regiment of doses. We want to convince them that we need a high dosage, so we need to pretend that we shoot up." Andy explained.

Madge looked down at her arms, "They can tell by looking at our arms that we are not shooters."

Andy stretched out his arm in front of himself. "We need to make little bruises up and down our arms." He demonstrated by pinching himself repeatedly up and down his arm.

Madge followed along, and after pinching their arms, they smacked the skin until tiny bruises began to appear.

Once they were confident that the nurses would believe their story by the marks on their arms they all three piled out of the truck. They still had to walk slowly, as both Andy and Madge were weak and queasy.

CHAPTER 16

When they walked in the front door of the clinic, there was a waiting room on the right side and a check in counter on the left. Andy approached the counter, while Madge and Nichole found a seat. Andy leaned against the counter to help hold him up and told the nurse that he and his wife were there for the first time. She handed him two clipboards with a form on each and instructed him to have a seat while they filled them out.

Andy sat down, and they went down the form together. Name...check. Date of birth...check. Weight, weight, ethnicity...check, check, and check. Address... Madge looked at Andy's form. "What do we put for address?" Andy looked from his form to hers. "Just leave it blank. If they tell us they need it, we can give my parents' address." The form went on asking about their drug use history and finally asked what drugs they were currently on and amount and frequency. Madge put the exact amount that she had been using, while Andy rounded up slightly to make sure he got a high dosage. They were both still feeling sick, but since they had completely emptied their stomachs before they arrived, they were able to maintain their composure, especially since they knew relief was on the way.

Andy carried the clipboards with completed forms back to the counter. He then returned to his seat where they waited for the nurse to call them in. There were about half a dozen other people in the waiting room, including a couple of children.

Nichole slid off the chair and walked over to a small station in the corner that was set up with kid's toys. Most of the toys were for much younger kids, but Nichole was bored and had limited access to toys in general. She sat down next to a four-year-old boy who was pushing a row of wooden trains back and forth. Nichole found the toy with the looping colored wires and chunky beads to glide across the wires from one end to the other. Nichole moved one head at a time across the wire puzzle, and, once she had all of the beads on one side, she attempted to glide an entire stack of beads at once.

While she was playing, a nurse called for both of her parents. Nichole stood and began to follow her parents through the door, but the nurse stopped her. "There are no children allowed in the back. Just stay in the waiting room, and, if you need something just ask the nurse at the counter. She will keep an eye on you." Nichole looked from her parents to the nurse and then to the nurse at the check-in counter. "It is okay," Madge reassured her. "We will be back before you know it." Accepting her mom's words, Nichole returned to the kids' corner in the waiting room and tried to find ways to entertain herself with wooden block puzzles. Finally, she found a small stack of children's books and found a spot to sit on the floor and read.

Behind the door, a second nurse took Andy to one station and the first nurse took Madge. They each sat on a hard chair while the nurses strapped blood pressure cuffs on to their arms and checked their blood pressure and pulse. They took their temperature with a disposable thermometer. Finally, they took turns weighing them on the one scale, and the nurses noted down everything. They checked the bruised track marks on their arms, and, much to Andy and Madge's relief, they were convincing enough for the nurses not to ask any extra questions. They then reviewed their answers on the forms they had filled out. They then explained to them how the methadone treatment would work.

They each received a prescribed dosage of methadone, and, the nurse told them if they come back regularly, they would continue to receive their doses as they gradually decreased to help curb their heroin addiction. Andy and Madge each signed the bottom of a second form saying that they understood their treatment plan and would begin treatment right away. With all this completed, the nurses directed them to a window where they handed the technician their completed forms, and they each received a small clear plastic cup with a bright green liquid inside.

Madge watched as Andy tipped his head back and poured the liquid in. He closed his eyes and stood frozen for a moment while he swallowed. Madge followed suit and drank her entire dosage. The relief was nearly instant. Their stomachs stopped churning mercilessly, and the anxiety slowed like a boiled pot of water, cooling down. As soon as they finished their dose, they left. They returned to the waiting room to find Nichole engrossed in a book. "Ready to go?" Andy called out to her. Nichole looked up and could immediately she the relief in her parents' faces. They were not sick anymore. She dropped the book on the floor and sprang to her feet to follow them out.

As soon as they stepped out the doors there was a woman handing out McDonald's gift certificates to everyone who walked by. They each accepted one. Andy and Madge were amazed at how hungry they were since they were not sick anymore. Each certificate was worth a couple dollars, which meant they could each get a burger and share fries and a drink.

As they drove to McDonalds Madge gathered up the bags and clothes that had been soiled with vomit, and they stopped to throw them away in one of the dumpsters that they used to scavenge. Nichole cradled her rabbit in her lap while feeding it a handful of grass that she had picked in front of the methadone clinic. They pulled into the McDonalds parking lot and when they walked into the fast food restaurant, they immediately went to the restrooms first to clean up. Once they were more presentable, they stood in line together. They has to use one coupon per order, so they figured out that Andy would order a burger and the drink, Madge would order a burger and the fries, and Nichole would be able to get her own kid's meal. One by one, they placed their orders and paid with the gift certificates.

While waiting for their food to be prepared, they found a booth table to sit at. As each order became available, Nichole ran to retrieve each order. They each ate their meals in silence. Andy and Madge could not remember ever enjoying food so much.

While they were finishing their food, and Nichole was opening the package for the toy in her kids' meal, another family sat in a booth near them. The mother and father were both yelling at their child. "What are you, stupid?" The child hung his head as his parents scolded him for whatever he had done to upset them so much. Nichole leaned behind her mom to see what was going on. "Sit down, Nichole." Andy told her. "But why are they being so mean to that boy? Aren't they his parents? I thought parents are supposed to be nice to their kids."

"They are supposed to," Madge reassured her, "but sometimes some parents forget that."

Nichole looked back and forth between her parents. "But you are never mean to me."

"Well," Andy took Nichole's hand in his from across the table, "we make a lot of mistakes every day, but we try to make sure that you always know that we love you."

"I know," Nichole nodded. "I finished all my food. Can I go play now?"

"Sure." Madge answered and slid out of the booth so that she could pass, and, she ran to the play area with the tunnels and slides and ball pit. While Nichole played, Andy and Madge tried to come up with a new plan.

"Well, dumpster diving and begging are no longer options now that Nichole is afraid of both," Madge reminded Andy.

"And your food stamps are never going to be enough to get us by," he added.

"In our condition and without an address, we will not even be able to get any jobs."

Andy leaned across the table with a razor blade in his hand and whispered, "I could pretend like this was in my burger and we could sue." Madge stared at him in disbelief. "That is the worst idea you have ever had!"

Back and forth, they discussed all of the scenarios that would not work.

While they talked, Nichole was trying to befriend the boy whose parents that been yelling at him. He seemed very nice, and that only gave Nichole more distress as to why his parents would be so mean to him. Nichole understood that her parents were not able to take the best care of her due to their addiction, but they were never mean to her.

Back inside, Andy had suggested that they start stealing and it made Madge extremely uncomfortable. "What if we get caught?" She asked. "I will do it, and you and Nichole just need to be the lookouts," he explained.

Madge leaned back in her seat and stared at him.

"We will have to do something! You know this methadone is going to wear off, and we will need another fix soon." Andy tapped his fingers on the table, desperate to get Madge to agree. "Plus, we will not be dealing with people face to face, so that will make it easier for Nichole."

Madge narrowed her eyes at him as she considered this. It is true she would do almost anything to make their situation at least a little more comfortable for their daughter. "Fine."

"Ha!" Andy pounded his fist on the table in victory.

"But," Madge decided to ask, "What things are we going to steal where we will not have to be face to face?"

"Things that are left unattended, like...car stereos." Andy replied as if the answer was so obvious.

CHAPTER 17

With a full stomach and a new plan, the family left McDonald's and drove to the field under the City water tower to park for the night. They set up their bed in the back with the tarp over the truck and fell asleep in record time.

The next morning Andy awoke early and thought about where he would hit first to grab a few car stereos to steal. He did not want to go when many people would be around, so either in the morning after people are at work but before they go to lunch or after lunch but before people started to leave. He next considered where they would go. He needed to find a place where the cars were nice enough to have stereos that he could sell but preferably without alarm systems. Finally, he decided that he would go to workplace parking lots where there are plenty of cars to choose from, and, if an alarm were to sound, it would take a while for anyone to realize which car it was. With his plan set up, he began waking Madge and Nichole. They all worked together to roll up their bedding and remove the tarp, and, within minutes, they were sitting in the front of the truck ready for their next task.

"Okay," Andy explained, "when I am getting the stereo, Madge, I will need you to be in the driver's seat in case we need to make a fast getaway."

Madge began to protest, "I do not even have my license! I do not know this area. I would not even know where to go,"

Andy stopped her, "I know. I know. You will not have to drive far. But if I am about to get caught, I will need to be able to jump into the back of the truck and for you to drive just far enough away so that we don't get caught. Then you can pull over, and I will take over."

Madge folded her arms in defeat, "Fine."

"And you," Andy turned to Nichole, "I will need you to be our lookout. If you see anyone watching us or coming toward us, I need you to yell out to me so I know to get away in time. Can you do that?"

Nichole looked in her father's pale blue eyes. He needed her, and she would not let him down. "I can do that." Andy hugged Nichole before shifting the truck into drive and heading out to scope out the best destination.

Andy pulled into a parking lot of a tall building and found a parking spot in the back. Employees were still arriving for the day, so they stayed in the car for an hour before Andy was confident that the coast was clear. He backed the truck out if the parking spot and pointed it down an aisle of cars. "Okay, Madge, I just need you to slowly follow me as I check the cars."

Madge's hands were already sweating. The last time she had driven was many years ago, and she had been in an accident where she decided that she never wanted to drive again. She walked around the truck and slid in the driver's seat. "It's okay, Mommy." Nichole rubbed her arm as Madge gripped the steering wheel. Andy walked over to the nearest car, leaned close with his hand cupped above his eyes to shield out the glare, and peered in the window. He saw a basic stereo system and decided that if he did not find anything better, he could come back to it. He strolled around to the next car and repeated his process. As he walked from car to car, Madge slowly released her foot off the brake and let the truck roll forward. Nichole turned in all directions to make sure nobody was watching them.

Finally, Andy stayed at one car longer. It had a stereo system that he knew would be easy to remove and should make a good sell, and, as far as he could tell the car did not have an alarm system. Andy removed a screwdriver from his coat pocket and gripped it with his hand inside the pocket so that he would not cut himself. He gave a final glance all around to make sure no one was coming, and then he smashed the screwdriver against the glass so that it shattered. He jostled the car and brushed the side of his jacket against the window frame to clear away the broken glass and then reached in unlock and open the door.

Using his screwdriver, he pried the stereo out of the console and ripped out the cords attaching it to the car. He stuffed the stereo into his jacket and slowly stepped out of the car. After another glance all around him, he casually walked to the truck and slipped into the driver's seat as Madge slid across to make room. This left Nichole on the passenger side, so she jumped over her mom as she slid over so they would each occupy their usual seats. Andy drove the truck out of the parking lot and down the road before any of them said a word. Finally, Andy broke the silence. "See! I told you that would work. Piece of cake."

Nichole caught on to her dad's enthusiasm. "And we did not have to see any mean people."

"That is right, Nichole! We will not go where people can mistreat us anymore. If we need something, we will find a way to get it ourselves."

Andy drove until they reached an area where he knew some people hung out looking for a good deal. He parked their truck in the alley and approached a group of men. Nichole watched out the window, and then he talked to them for several minutes before finally pulling the stereo out of his jacket and showing it to one of them. They talked some more, negotiating a price that they finally agreed on, and the man counted out a handful of bills and handed it to Andy. Andy took the cash and shoved it into his pocket before he shook the man's hand and walked back to the truck.

"We will have enough to get a hit!" Andy announced to Madge as he jumped in the truck and sped away.

Andy drove to his drug dealer's house and knocked on the door. Within a few minutes, he was back with a small ball of heroin. They drove to a park, where Nichole played with Chloe in the grass while her parents smoked the heroin.

They repeated this routine for several days, and each became more comfortable with their roles. Although after a while, they began to become more desperate and less alert.

One day Andy pulled in the alley behind a strip mall where the employees parked their cars. They each took their positions, and Andy checked inside a few cars before settling on one. He thrust the screwdriver in the window and as it shattered the door to one of the businesses burst open. "What do you think you are doing to my car?" A man in a white karate uninform with a black belt screamed as he ran toward him. Andy bolted for the truck, he gripped the side as he flipped his feet up over his head and he landed in the back of the truck. Madge pressed the gas pedal all of the way to the floor, and the tires screeched as they sped away. The karate instructor ran after them, but Madge made a sharp turn on the first road and drove a few blocks away before making another turn. Andy gripped the side of the truck to keep from sliding around. At last, Madge rolled to a stop, Andy jumped out, and everyone returned to their regular seats. Andy chuckled as he took his seat, "I did not even realize that that was a karate studio."

"That is not funny!" Madge yelled at him. "He could have killed you! And he has probably already called the cops!"

Andy tried to reassure Madge that they had really gotten away with it, but she was not convinced. "If you are going to steal things, you need to find something that is not so risky."

Although he did not like to admit it, Andy had to agree with her. One of the men had mentioned to him when he was selling stereos that they were also in the market for bicycles. They had even mentioned a few brands that they would pay more for. "Okay, okay. No more stereos. We will start trying to find bicycles we can grab."

"And you won't have to break into cars." Madge added.

Nichole looked over her shoulder at the bike. "Can I have a bike, Daddy?"

"Maybe," Andy answered, "if we find one in your size, but we might need to sell it if we need the money." Andy knew that every single bike they took they would have to sell, but he avoided disappointing his daughter.

Andy drove to the alley where he had sold the stereos and looked for the man who was interested in bikes. He was not in the usual spot, so Andy asked around and found him hanging out in the alley behind the pawnshop. Andy rolled the bike to where he was standing and tried to negotiate a price. The man asked where Andy had stolen the bike from but Andy claimed that the bike was not stolen, but that a friend had given it to him. The man did not believe him but accepted his answer because he preferred to do business with people who were smart about what information they shared. He knew that Andy had stolen the bike because otherwise he would have sold it inside the pawnshop for a better price, but they keep records of all sales and purchases in case the police ask for a report.

They, once again, settled into their new routine of scouting for and stealing bicycles. Andy was the runner, Nichole was the lookout, and Madge was the getaway driver.

One day while out scouting for bicycles, Nichole spotted a bike leaning against the side of a garage. "Look there, Daddy!" She pointed. "It looks like a good one." Andy slowed the truck as the passed the house with a blue and black Huffy propped against the garage. "That does look like a good one," Andy agreed. He drove the truck around the block and stopped a few houses away from their target. He looked over to Madge and Nichole. "Ready?" They both nodded, and Andy and Madge each got out of the car, and, Madge slid into the driver's seat, while Andy walked toward the bike. Nichole watched the house, checking to see if anybody was around. She glanced up and down the street to make sure nobody was watching.

When Andy reached the bike, he stood it up from the wall and, when he did, a bag of cans fell off the handle and crashed to the ground. Andy froze at the disturbance. When he thought nobody had heard, he began to push the bike down the driveway. When he reached the middle of the driveway, the garage door swung open. "Hey, stop!" A man came running after Andy. Andy pushed the bike faster, running alongside it, but the man was gaining on him. Madge and Nichole were screaming at him from the truck to hurry. While he was running, Andy jumped and swung his leg over the side of the bike and peddled as fast as he could. "Go! Go! Go!" He waved to Madge as he whizzed passed them on the truck.

Madge stomped on the gas, and they sped away after Andy. Once Madge caught up to him, she slowed enough for him to slide off the bike, heave it into the back of the truck, and jump in the back with it. Once again, Madge sped away and turned down the block. Andy tapped on the window from the back of the truck. "Pull over and I will drive!" He yelled. Madge slammed on the brakes, and Andy's face pressed against the glass. As soon as they came to a stop, Madge shifted into park and climbed across the seat, over Nichole, as Andy scampered in the driver's seat and drove away. Andy did not stop until they were several miles away and after winding up and down various streets, in case, some decided to follow them.

CHAPTER 18

When they reached the downtown pawnshop, Andy hoisted the bike out of the back of their truck and pushed it down the alley next door to the shop. As usual, there was a group of men hanging out in the alley, but Andy could not find his usual contact. After asking around, he found out that the police had arrested him the day before. One of the other men there asked Andy about the bike and even made an offer on the bike. Andy agreed so that he could rid himself of the bike before the owner had a chance to report it stolen.

After selling the bike, Andy drove the truck to his dealer and made a purchase. They drove to the park, where Nichole played while he and Madge finished their hit.

Nichole ran across the playground with her rabbit on its leash. She held it on her lap as she slid down the slide, and, when she got tired, she laid on the grass watching it nibble away at the plants.

Sometimes Nichole thought about school, but she knew if she said anything, her dad would claim that he would take her to enroll in school "tomorrow."

While playing on the jungle gym, Nichole noticed a group of kids walking by in costumes. A little boy was dressed as a superhero, a little girl wore a princess dress, and another girl was in a long black dress with a pointy witch's hat. Children carried either a bag or a basket with them. Nichole realized it must be Halloween! She ran to the truck where her parents were just coming off their high.

"Guess what!" Nichole opened the passenger door and climbed across her mother's lap. "Today is Halloween!"

Andy and Madge looked around as Nichole pointed out all of the children in costumes.

"Can I go trick or treating?" She asked pleading.

"What would you wear?" Andy looked down at her.

Nichole thought for a moment. She did not have any costumes, and they did not have money to buy a whole outfit.

"Maybe we can check the ninety nine cent store." Madge suggested.

"Yeah!" Nichole agreed.

Andy nodded, but continued to sit there while the effects of the heroin subsided enough for him to drive.

At last, Andy drove the truck away from the park, and they found their way to a ninety-nine cent store. Andy waited in the truck while Madge and Nichole walked in hand in hand.

They strolled up and down the aisles before settling on a headband with cat ears and a simple makeup kit to draw cat features on her face.

"With your face dressed up, nobody will notice whether or not you are wearing a full costume." Madge explained.

Nichole was too excited about being able to go trick or treating to worry about her costume.

At the cashier, Madge paid the two dollars for the costume supplies, and they walked back to the truck.

"What did you get?" Andy asked as soon as they returned to the truck.

Nichole held the bag open for Andy to look inside. "I am going to be a kitty!"

She pulled the headband out of the bag and slid it on. She gathered her feet under herself on the seat so that she could see in the rearview mirror. Upon seeing her reflection with the cat ears, Nichole beamed.

"Okay, now let's make your kitty face." Madge took the makeup kit out of the bag.

Using the small applicator stick, Madge drew black lines across Nichole's cheeks for whiskers. She then colored her nose pink and drew two curved black lines under her nose to look like a cat's mouth; she even made a pink tongue sticking out.

"So what do you think?" Madge sat back while Nichole looked in the mirror again.

"I am a kitty!" Nichole hugged her mom and turned to her dad to show him her face.

"Ha, ha. Yes, you are." Andy agreed.

"Can I go trick or treating now?" Nichole sat down in her seat and buckled her seatbelt to show them that she was ready to go right now.

Andy nodded and drove the truck out of the parking lot. They drove around until they found a neighborhood where several other kids were already trick or treating. "This looks like a good spot." Andy parked the truck on the side of the street, and they all three climbed out.

They walked down the sidewalk holding hands in a line, with Nichole in the middle. At the first house, they walked up to the door with her and told her to knock on the door. Nichole stepped close and reached out her small fist to knock three times. The door swung open, and a woman holding a bowl of candy stood in front of her.

"Treat or Treat!" Nichole called out.

"Oh, look! It's a cat!" the woman exclaimed as she reached into the bowl and handed Nichole a candy bar.

Nichole smiled the biggest smile her mouth could make. "Thank you."

"You are welcome," the woman answered before closing the door again.

They continued through the neighborhood knocking on doors, collecting candy. By the end of the night, Nichole had stuffed her pockets with candy and had gathered the hem of her shirt in her hands to hold the rest of the candy in it. When they reached the end of the neighborhood, they noticed that there were not any other children out anymore and decided to stop as well.

Back in the truck, they drove to the field under the water tower, and Andy and Madge set up their bed for the night, while Nichole sorted through her candy. She piled all of the chocolates together, all of the suckers together, all of the hard candies together, and all of the bubble gums together. She picked out all of the candies that had peanuts or coconut or anything else she did not like and made a pile for her mom, who did like those things.

Once the bed was completed, Madge called for Nichole to come to bed. Before going to bed, Nichole moved her piles of candy to the dashboard so that Chloe would not eat them during the night. She then took a couple of pieces in her fist and crawled through the rear window into the bed of the truck where her parents were already waiting. She handed them each a piece of candy, and she slid under the blankets between them.

"Thank you, Baby." Madge took the Snickers that Nichole handed to her.

"Yes, thank you." Andy accepted the KitKat.

Nichole grinned as she popped a Tootsie Roll in her mouth.

"Are we going to do a bedtime story tonight?" Madge turned on her side to look at her daughter.

Nichole nodded as she chewed her Tootsie Roll before swallowing it.

Nichole began, "Once upon a time, there was Nichole. She had a big house that looked like a castle. Many other kids lived in her castle with her because she rescued them and gave them a home. She also had lots of animals because she rescued them too."

Andy turned on his side also to pay attention to the story. "What adventure are you going to go on this time?"

Nichole thought for a moment before turning to Madge. "Are there any animals that I do not have yet?"

Madge thought back over all of the stories they told each night. "You already had dogs, and cats, and rabbits, and horses. You have goats and chickens and cows."

Nichole nodded, "And I have a tiger and a lion and a zebra."

"Do you have a giraffe?" Andy chimed in.

"No, I do not have a giraffe!" Nichole answered and so she continued her story. "One day Nichole was at the zoo, and, when she got to the giraffe cage she saw that the giraffe did not have very much room to move around, and it looked sad. Nichole asked the zookeeper if they had a bigger cage for the giraffe so that it could have more room like in the wild. The zookeeper said that was all they had and they might have to put the giraffe to sleep because it could not live much longer in the small cage, and they could not send in the wild because it had lived at the zoo since it was a baby."

"Nichole told the zookeeper that she had her own castle. She told him that she had lots of land for the giraffe where it could live happily. The zookeeper asked the owner of the zoo, and they agreed to let the giraffe go live with Nichole. They took the giraffe in a giant truck and drove it to Nichole's castle. When they let it out, it ran in the giant field. The giraffe was now happy, and Nichole promised that she would take good care of it, and they could come visit anytime. Now Nichole was happy, the giraffe was happy, and the zoo was happy that the giraffe had a good new home. The end."

Madge smiled at Nichole with her cat makeup still on her face. "That was a wonderful story."

Nichole turned to look at her dad and found that he was already fast asleep. She giggled, "My story made daddy fall asleep."

Madge laughed with her. "Yes, but we should get some sleep too."

Nichole nodded and drew the blankets up under her chin and closed her eyes until she drifted off to sleep.

CHAPTER 19

As their life on the streets continued to progress, they settled into the routine of scouting for bikes to steal, selling them, getting drugs, getting food, playing in the park, and sleeping.

One day they were driving through a familiar neighborhood looking for bikes when Andy noticed a police car in his rear view mirror. "There is a cop behind us. Make sure that you have your seat belts on, and, if we play it smart, they will not pull us over."

Nichole already had her seat belt on, but Madge slowly reached for hers and pulled it across her lap. Nichole reached for her mom's seat belt and helped her click it in the buckle.

Andy took a turn onto another street, but he saw the cop make the same turn behind him. "Yep, they are following us." Beads of sweat began to form on his brow.

Andy continued to drive, making sure that he was staying within the speed limit and obeying all traffic laws.

The cop continued to follow them.

Andy's hands began to shake as he gripped the steering wheel. He made another turn onto a small street, and, as soon as he turned, the lights on top of the cop car flashed and swirled.

Andy cursed as he slowed the car to a stop. "We tell them nothing. Hide anything that might make them suspicious. If we get busted, they will take Nichole away."

Madge and Nichole nodded and checked around them to make sure that they did not have anything around that might get them in trouble.

Andy watched in the rear view mirror as the police officer slowly walked toward them. When the cop reached his window, Andy slowly turned the knob to roll down his window. "Is there a problem, officer?"

"License and registration." The cop responded.

Andy fumbled through his pockets until he found one of the old driver's licenses that he had stolen. He had long ago memorized the information on the I.D. in case he ever needed it. He handed the license to the cop.

Taking the license, he repeated, "And registration."

Andy leaned across the seat and popped open the glove compartment. He leafed through the papers pretending to look for the registration. "It looks like it has gone missing."

The cop looked in the truck at the three of them, turned, and walked back to his car.

Andy cursed again as soon as the cop was out of earshot.

Madge began to panic. "This is it. We need to show them that they cannot separate us from Nichole."

"They do not have anything against us yet." Andy tried to appear calm.

They sat in the car for several minutes before another cop car drove past and turned around in front of them to park across the street.

The first cop got back out of his car and walked back to the truck. "I am going to need to ask you a few questions."

"No problem," Andy answered, "we have nothing to hide."

"I am afraid I will need to talk to you individually." The cop stepped back. "Please step out of the car."

Andy turned and looked at Madge and Nichole. He gave them a wink before opening his door and stepping out of the car.

Madge and Nichole watched through the back window as the cop walked Andy to the curb where he had Andy sit down while they talked. He asked him a series of questions related to where they live, what he does for a living, and if he was using any drugs.

Without hesitating, Andy answered every single question with a made up story of how they lived nearby, and that he was a mechanic, and no, he was not under the influence of any drugs.

While the first cop was talking to Andy, two more cops got out of the second cop car and approached the truck. A female officer approached Madge's door and asked her to follow her to a place across the street where she could question her. The third cop invited Nichole to come out of the truck and stood with her in front of the truck while he asked her questions.

They had never rehearsed what they would say in case this ever happened, but Nichole knew how things were supposed to be, and so she made up a story about how she was out of school for the day because she had a doctor's appointment. She even told him about her bedroom and how she had it decorated. When he asked about school, Nichole told him that she was enrolled in Linda Vista Elementary

School, which was where she last attended. When the officer asked her the name of her teacher, she gave him the name of the teacher she had had the year before.

After several minutes of questioning, two of the cops gathered to discuss what was going on while the third searched through the truck. As soon as he opened the door, he spotted the rabbit sitting on the floor chewing on a lettuce leaf sitting on a McDonald's burger wrapper.

He looked under the seats, in the glove compartment, behind the seat, and, when he slide his hand along the cracks of the seat, he found the folded pieces of used aluminum foil, the lighter, and the straws. He gathered the items together and took them to show the others office. Drug paraphernalia alone was enough to arrest them.

He showed one officer while the other was at his car talking on the radio. They had called the school Nichole told them she attended, and they just received word that she was, in fact, not enrolled there and had not been for several months. They finally all gathered to discuss their plan. They had to call for a third cop car since they knew they would be arresting both adults and taking the child away separately.

The first officer approached Andy where he remained sitting on the curb and read him his rights, and then he handcuffed him. The third cop car arrived and Andy walked with the officer and climbed into the car. His plan was to pretend as if he did not know what was going on and deny any charges against him. He hoped that since he used a false I.D. that they would not see that he had a record, and then he would get out within a few days.

With just Madge and Nichole left behind, Madge prayed that they were only taking Andy, and that she and Nichole would be able to go free.

The female cop approached Madge where she was also sitting on the curb, and, as she pulled out the handcuffs and began to read her her rights, Madge stood and tried to run to Nichole. The officer grabbed her arm and pulled her back. "NO!" Madge screamed as she struggled to get out of the officer's grip to reach her daughter.

The officer held and twisted her arm against her back until she stopped struggling. The officer reprimanded her, "Is this really how you want your daughter to see you?" Madge looked up and saw the terrified expression on her daughter's face. She stopped struggling and stood limply, with tears streaming down her face, and the officer cinched the cuffs on her.

Back at the truck, the third officer walked Nichole back to one of the cars. Before instructing her to get in the car, he opened the trunk and pulled out a stuffed animal. It was exactly like the teddy bear that Nichole had when they first became homeless, and she had lost it somewhere along the way. The officer handed the bear to Nichole, and she took it suspiciously. "What is going to happen to my bunny?" Nichole asked, as the officer opened the passenger door and helped her into the seat.

"We will take good care of it," He replied.

With Madge in one car and Nichole in the other, the two officers met in the middle of the street, where they talked briefly and switched places so that the woman officer drove the car that Nichole was in and the man took Madge.

Madge continued to cry as she watched her daughter riding away in the other cop car.

Nichole sat motionless in her seat clutching the teddy bear, and the woman officer climbed into the car beside her. "Are you scared?"

Nichole did not speak but just shook her head from side to side. Andy had taught Nichole how to conceal her feelings so that people could not take advantage of her.

The officer continued to make small talk but Nichole only answered with nods and shrugs. On the way, they pulled into the McDonald's drive-thru. "Are you hungry?" the officer asked.

Nichole shrugged her shoulders and looked at the floor.

They pulled through the line around the restaurant and the officer ordered a kid's meal. She set it on the seat next to Nichole and continued driving. Nichole eyed the bag before reaching in and pulling out a few French fries. She nibbled on them, still without saying a word to the officer.

CHAPTER 20

They drove on the freeway for a few miles before exiting and pulling into the parking lot for Orangewood Children's Home.

The officer walked Nichole inside. There was a woman waiting for them when they walked in. She smiled and introduced herself to Nichole. The officer shook her hand and said "Goodbye" to Nichole before turning and leaving her there. Nichole watched the officer leave but remained standing in the middle of the room with the woman she had just met. Nichole was not paying much attention to her and had already forgotten her name.

The woman walked Nichole through the building and out a door. When they stepped outside, Nichole looked all around. There were many buildings around them. Off to her right there was a playground, where groups of kids were playing. The woman took Nichole's hand and guided her to another building, where she helped her pick out some clean clothes in her size, as well as some new shoes. Before Nichole could change into her new clothes, the woman had to look at her arms, legs, back, and stomach. The woman had to write down if she had any marks or bruises on her. The only marks Nichole had were some scabs on her knees from falling in her roller blades.

After Nichole changed into her clean clothes, the woman walked her to another building. Inside there were several other girls her age and a few adults. One woman approached them when they walked in and introduced herself. Again, Nichole was not interested and did not reply or bother remembering her name. The women talked for a minute before the first lady knelt down in front of Nichole. "This is going to be your new home now. They will show you your room and help you get settled."

Nichole nodded and turned to look around the building. There were stairs that led up to a long row of doors. Downstairs there was a room with couches and a TV. In the kitchen, a woman was cooking.

The woman who had greeted her guided Nichole up the steps and showed her to her room. There were three beds set up in the room along the walls. Two beds had colorful blankets and pillows, and the third bed had a basic white sheet and simple pillow. The woman motioned to the third bed. "This is for you. You get to have two roommates. I am sure you will all become friends."

The woman looked at Nichole, waiting for a response. Nichole shrugged and set her teddy bear on the bed.

That night Nichole met her new roommates. One of the girls had been homeless like she was, except the girl had been only with her mom, and they did not have a car or anything, so they had to sleep on the ground at night. The other girl told Nichole how her mom's boyfriend used to hurt her, so she was taken here. Nichole shared her experiences with the girls, and they did seem like they could all be friends. That night as Nichole lay in her bed waiting for sleep, she thought about her parents. She knew that they were in jail, and that they would not be able to get their drugs. She remembered what it was like watching them going through withdrawals, and she wished that they would be able to get better soon.

The next day Nichole woke to an alarm that rung through the whole house. When she walked out of her room, girls were scurrying every single direction. Nichole walked to the bathroom and found that someone was already in it. "You have to wait your turn," one of the older girls told her and pointed to a sign-up list to use the bathroom. Nichole walked away, and one of her roommates spotted her. She ran up to Nichole and put her arm around her shoulder. "There is a smaller bathroom downstairs, and the older girls do not like to use it because it does not have a mirror."

Nichole followed her new friend down the stairs and found the small half bathroom empty. She went to the bathroom, washed her hands, and then found her way to breakfast.

After breakfast, one of the housemothers called out that it was almost time to go. It turned out it was Sunday, and there was a chapel on campus that they were required to attend. Nichole had been to church before with her grandparents. Her mom's parents had taken her to a church where they sang slow hymns and had flannel board stories in Sunday School. She had also been to church with her dad's parents at their Pentecostal church, where they sang fast gospel songs and you clapped along. Neither of her parents ever went to church. In fact, according to her father, churches only brainwash you, and the only reason he ever considered going was in the event where they might give them money or something.

Nevertheless, she walked in the line of girls to the chapel. Immediately it was different from the churches she had attended. This was a Catholic church. The priest talked for a long time, and Nichole could not understand most of what he was saying. The seats were long wooden pews, and, after sitting for a while, it began to hurt her legs. Nichole decided that she agreed with her parents: Going to church was not for her.

The next day was Monday, and one of the housemothers walked Nichole to the on-campus school. This was the first time since she arrived that Nichole was excited about something. It had been so long since she had gone to school and she had pestered her dad about it so many times, and now she was finally going. She told her housemother, "I will be in the fourth grade this year."

When they arrived at the school, the housemother took her into a classroom that had about ten other kids in it. The teacher explained that the class was for second, third, and fourth grades. Nichole's shoulders dropped in disappointment. She was finally in school but with kids much younger. Since Thanksgiving was approaching, the teacher read them a storybook about pilgrims and the ships that sailed with Columbus. Nichole did not understand the connection, but she participated in the activities anyway.

That night in bed, Nichole cried herself to sleep. She missed her parents, she missed her rabbit, and the only activity that she had been looking forward to at the children's home was a complete disappointment.

The next day after school, her housemother called her out of her room. "You have a visitor."

Nichole followed one of the office staff to the front building. As soon as she walked in her Granny, Grandpa, and Aunt Karyn greeted her with hugs. Nichole was so excited to see them and they told her that they were working to get her to be able to come live with them. She asked about her Aunt Kathy and Uncle Mike and her cousins Kenny and Katie. Unfortunately, her cousins were too young to visit her there, and so they just planned to see her when she came home with Granny and Grandpa.

Nichole could not be more excited! If she could not be with her parents, at least she should be with family.

The next day at school, Nichole was playing on the swings with one of her friends during recess.

"Did you hear that Emily is not going home, even though they told her she would be?" Her friend asked her.

"No. But I am going to be going home with my grandparents soon. They came to visit me yesterday and told me so," Nichole answered.

"Oh, people say that all of the time, and then it does not happen."

Nichole thought about her friends answer, and she looked at the fence surrounding the field and playground where they were playing. The fence was the only barrier separating them from the outside.

Nichole drug her feet on the ground to stop her swing. "Well, if I do not get to leave by next week, I am going to run away."

Her friend stopped her swing beside her. "How are you going to do that?"

Nichole pointed to the tree on the far end of the field near the fence. "One day during recess, I will play by that tree. And then when recess is over, I will hide behind the tree until everyone goes inside, and then I will just climb over the fence."

"But what will you do out there by yourself?"

"My dad taught me how to take care of myself."

Her friend shook her head. The school bell rang, and they walked back to their class together.

CHAPTER 21

Throughout the rest of the week, Nichole continued to plan her escape in case she was not able to go live with her grandparents.

Before the week was over, one of the workers from the office came to Nichole's room. "You have court today. Gather your belongings in case you do not return. We will leave in thirty minutes."

Nichole looked up at the woman standing in the doorway of her room and realized that she was talking to her. Nichole stood up from where she was sitting on her bed and looked around the room. She did not have much to gather, but she grabbed her teddy bear and the few clothes she had collected since living there. Nichole stuffed everything into a plastic grocery bag. Within five minutes, she was ready.

Nichole carried her belongings down the staircase with her and looked around for her roommates. They were both sitting on the couch watching TV. When she walked up to them, they saw that she was holding her clothes and teddy bear. "Are you leaving today?" one asked.

"I think so," Nichole sat on the couch between them, and set her clothes and bear at her feet. "They said I have court today. I think that it is to decide if I can go live with my grandparents."

Her friends took turns giving her a hug, and then they sat together watching cartoons until the worker returned, and Nichole walked out with her.

For the first time since the police officer had brought Nichole to Orangewood, she was on the outside of the campus. A few other kids also had to go to court that day, and they had a couple of staff to take them there. The Family Court building was just next door, so they walked in a single-file line to the building.

The worker who had brought Nichole checked her file to figure out which courtroom was reviewing her case. "Come this way." They walked to the elevators, and the worker pressed the "up" button.

The doors finally opened, and they stepped inside and ascended a few floors before getting off.

Nichole followed the worker down the hallways. As they walked to her courtroom, Nichole knew then they were at the right one because there waiting in the hallway were her grandparents and Aunt Karyn. Nichole ran to them and hugged them each.

The Orangewood worker caught up to Nichole and shook their hands. They exchanged some brief small talk about how the courtroom had not opened yet, and that they would call her case when they were ready.

Nichole sat on the wooden bench in the hallway between her Granny and Grandpa while they waited.

A man in a dark blue suit and blue striped tie came down the hallway and looked at Nichole. "Are you Miss Carpenter?"

Nichole looked up at him and then at her grandparents before deciding to answer. She often became shy when approached by strangers, so she just nodded.

"I am your attorney for this case. May I talk to you privately for a moment?"

Nichole looked again at her grandparents for reassurance. "It is okay, Nichole. We will be right here."

Nichole slid off the bench and followed the attorney to another spot on the bench further down where no one else was sitting and where no one could hear.

"So, Miss Carpenter, do you understand what today's hearing is about?"

Nichole shrugged her shoulders. No one had told her anything, but she figured it was so that she could go to live with her grandparents until her mom and dad got out of jail.

"What is happening today is that the court will be deciding if it would be suitable for you to be placed in your grandparents' temporary custody. That means that you would go to live with them and they would take care of you instead of your parents or Orangewood. You are currently a ward of the state, and so they will be deciding what is best for you. Of course, they want to know what you want, as that will have a strong influence on their decision."

He paused and looked at Nichole to see if she understood.

"I want to live with my mom and dad."

He nodded, "I understand that. However, at this time the courts have deemed your parents unfit, especially since they are currently incarcerated."

Nichole nodded. She knew that was the case, but she figured it was worth a shot.

"Since you cannot be released in your parents' custody at this time, what would you like to do? Would you like to remain at Orangewood or with a foster family, or would you like to be placed with your family?"

"I want to be with my family..." Nichole trailed off.

He eyed her suspiciously. "Is there any reason that you would not want to live with your grandparents?"

Nichole remembered the stories her dad had told her about church and religion. "I want to be with them, but I do not want to have to go to their church."

Her attorney scribbled some notes on his legal pad and was about to respond, when an officer in uniform opened the courtroom door and called out for her case. Nichole and her attorney both stood. He turned to her, "You just stay out here, and I will go and tell the judge everything you told me. You can sit and wait here, and I will come and get you when the judge has an answer."

Nichole nodded and walked with him to where her grandparents stood. He paused and shook her hand before going into the courtroom with her grandparents. Nichole then watched them walk into the courtroom, and the door closed behind them. Nichole returned to the bench where her Aunt Karyn was still waiting and sat next to her.

Inside the courtroom, her attorney reviewed Nichole's case and shared with the judge her desire to be in her grandparents' custody, and then he even shared with the judge her request to not be required to attend their church.

The judge questioned her grandparents about their ability to provide and care for Nichole. After several minutes of questioning, he announced that he had reached a decision and asked for the attorney to bring Nichole into the courtroom.

Her attorney turned and walked out the large wooden doors and motioned for Nichole to come inside. She picked up her bag with her clothes and teddy bear and followed him into the courtroom. They walked up to a table facing the judge.

The judge looked down at Nichole. "Miss Carpenter, we are here today to determine if it is in your best interest to be placed in the custody of your grandparents. You attorney has shared with the court that it is your expressed desire to live with them. Is that correct?"

Nichole looked around the room. This certainly was not her first time in a courtroom. She had been in many over the years but had never talked to a judge before. Every single other time she had been sitting on the bench in the back with her mom, while her father was the one being questioned or sentenced. In fact, she had taken many naps on such benches. She remembered waking to see her father being led away in handcuffs, and the next time she saw him was in a concrete room with a wall of windows and cement stools with telephones to talk to one another from either side of the window. She remembered seeing him in brightly colored jumpsuits.

"Miss Carpenter?" The judge's voice brought Nichole back to the present.

"Yes, I want to live with my Granny and Grandpa."

"Very good," the judge replied. "I do see that you expressed one condition to your desire to being in their custody, and I am afraid I will not be able to enforce it. If you are in your grandparents' custody you are likely to have to attend church with them if they so insist. Is that acceptable to you?"

Nichole looked over her shoulder at her grandparents sitting and watching her from the side. She thought about returning to Orangewood where she would have to attend a church she already did not like anyway, and she decided that if she had to choose between the two, that she would definitely prefer to be with her family. "I guess that is okay."

"All right. Then at this time, the State will award temporary custody of Nichole Anne Carpenter to Owen and Carolyn Carpenter. A follow-up hearing will be scheduled for six months from today's date, at which time the courts will review this case. Nichole's biological parents will be offered monitored visitation when they are no longer incarcerated and will be required to complete a series of drug rehabilitation and parenting classes. This court is dismissed."

The judge dropped his gavel on the table and rose from his seat. As he walked out the side door of the courtroom, Nichole's grandparents ran to the front and gathered her in their arms.

"You can finally come home now," her Granny was crying as she held her close to her.

Grandpa placed his hand gently on her back as they all walked out of the courtroom together. They told her Aunt Karyn, who was waiting, that they would all be going home together. "Praise God!" she cried out.

Nichole was glad to be going home with family, but she still was not sure about having to go to their church with them.

CHAPTER 22

Nichole walked with her Aunt Karyn and grandparents out of the courtroom and to the car. She sat in the back with her aunt, while her granny sat in front of her, and her grandpa drove.

Nichole watched out the window as they drove down the streets and onto the freeway. She was familiar with the area and watched as they past neighborhoods where she and her parents had dumpster dived. They drove passed the McDonald's where she went with her parents and where the police officer had taken her when they had separated her from her parents. They drove past the grocery store where she and her father had used to beg in front of. Then they drove up the hill, and Nichole knew that if they kept going over the hill, that would go to Looney's Donuts. Nichole recognized the street where they turned and knew that as they pulled into the long driveway, that just a couple blocks away sat the house that she used to live in with her parents before they became homeless.

Nichole thought about her mom and dad and figured they were probably not getting sick anymore, and maybe they would be getting enough food to eat, and that they did not have to try to find a place to sleep every single night.

Finally, her grandpa pulled the car to a stop in front of their house. "Home at last," he called out and looked at her through his rear view mirror.

Nichole smiled at him, and then he gave her a reassuring wink and nod.

She gathered her bag in her hands and followed them into the house.

As soon as they walked in, Zamu, her aunt's dog, began circling and dancing with excitement that everyone was home. When Zamu saw Nichole, she stopped and sniffed her, trying to determine if she was going to accept her into her home.

"It is okay, Zamu. You remember Nichole, right?" Her aunt knelt on the floor next to the dog and stroked her back, while taking Nichole's hand on hers. Zamu sniffed their hands together and licked her aunt's hand.

Nichole wondered if they ever figured out that she and her dad had broken in to take their mail. It seemed like Zamu remembered.

"She will get used to you again," Aunt Karyn reassured her. "Let's get you settled in your room."

They walked together through the living room and into the bedroom. "We will be sharing a bed while you are here. Are you okay with that?"

Nichole nodded. She did not say so, but she preferred to sleep with someone. She could not remember the last time she had had to sleep in a room by herself, and the thought of having to sleep alone frightened her. Nichole found herself thankful that her aunt was living with her grandparents at this time, and that they only had two bedrooms.

Her aunt pulled open a drawer of her dresser. "I cleared out this drawer for you in case you got to come home with us today."

Nichole took her bag and emptied her clothes in the drawer.

"How about tomorrow we go to the store, and you can pick out some more outfits? Would you like that?"

"Okay." Nichole answered. She could not remember the last time she had bought clothes from a store.

As Nichole was closing the dresser drawer, she heard the front door open and close. She walked out of the room, and she saw that it was her cousin Katie. "Hey, welcome back!"

"Thanks." Nichole answered. Her cousin was only a few months older than she was and lived right next door.

"Do you want to come see the new rabbits?" Katie asked.

"Sure," Nichole answered, and she followed her cousin out the door.

Her grandparents' house was actually the guesthouse next to her Aunt Kathy and Uncle Mike's house. There was a large grassy yard between them. There was a fence behind the houses. Walking through the gate led to a barn and arena with horses, chickens, and rabbits. Most of the horses were not theirs. They rented the stalls to people who did not have a place to keep their horses.

Nichole followed her cousin through the gate and past the barn. There was a stack of cages two high and four wide with eight cages. Inside each cage was a different rabbit. Katie named off each one and opened the doors to pet them before moving to the next one. Nichole followed quietly behind her, petting the rabbits when Katie did. When they reached the end of the cages, Katie stopped. "So, are you ready to see the new rabbit?"

Nichole nodded, and, as they turned toward another cage by itself, Nichole noticed her grandparents, aunts, and uncle standing in the barn watching them. She figured they must be happy to have her there, and she continued to follow her cousin. Katie knelt in front of the cage. "So, what do you think?"

Nichole knelt down beside her and looked into the cage. The rabbit was brown and white. It was nibbling on a piece of straw. "It kind of looks like…"

Nichole looked up at Katie, who was grinning widely at her. She turned and looked back at the rabbit. "Wait! Is this? Is this my rabbit Chloe?"

Katie giggled, "It is about time you figured it out, Dodo."

Nichole turned and looked at her grandparents, who were also smiling widely. She lifted the latch on the cage and swung the door open. She reached inside and lifted the rabbit out. She held her to her face and rubbed Chloe's fur against her cheek. "It is really you. You are okay. Everything is going to be okay." A tear fell down Nichole's cheek as she hugged her rabbit to her.

After a moment, she put Chloe back into her cage and latched the door closed. Then she rose to her feet and ran to her grandpa and granny. She flung her arms around them both and hugged them with all of her strength.

They then all walked back to the house, where Granny had prepared a welcome home meal for Nichole. They had macaroni and cheese made with real cheese, and mashed potatoes with melted butter and gravy. When everyone had finished eating her grandpa leaned his chair back on its rear legs and stretched his arms out. "Now, how about some dessert?"

Granny rose from the table and went to the fridge. Aunt Karyn went with her to the kitchen to grab a stack of bowls and spoons. Granny returned to the table with a tub of cottage cheese and a large opened can of sliced peaches with a fork sitting in it. Grandpa went first, using a spoon to scoop out a large heap of cottage cheese into his bowl, and then he used the fork to pick out several peach slices and set them on top of the cottage cheese. They each passed the bowls around and dished out their dessert. Nichole looked around the table at her family and was very glad that she had decided to come home with them instead of staying at Orangewood.

That night Nichole slept peacefully in the bed with her Aunt Karyn, and, when she awoke the next morning, she could already smell breakfast cooking.

She climbed out of bed and walked into the kitchen. Her Aunt Karyn was standing in front of the stove with a frying pan. She looked up when Nichole walked in the room. "Good morning, Sunshine! Are you hungry?"

Nichole nodded and took a seat at the bar where she could watch.

"I am making chocolate chip pancakes. How does that sound?"

Nichole answered by smiling and licking her lips.

Aunt Karyn laughed and took a plate from the cupboard. She scooped two pancakes off the pan and onto the plate. She set the plate in front of Nichole. She slid a jar of warm syrup across the counter to Nichole.

Nichole ate every single bite of her breakfast and even proceeded to lick the syrup off the plate when she was done.

As Nichole licked her plate, the phone rang and Aunt Karyn stood up from the table where she had joined Nichole and answered it.

"Hello!"

Nichole looked up to where her aunt stood and watched her.

On the other side of the call a recorded operator's voice said, "This is a collect call from..." a voice interrupted the recording "this is Madge..." the recording continued, "to accept this call and all applicable charges press 1."

Karyn reached for the keypad and pressed the number 1.

The phone beeped a couple of times, and then Karyn could hear noise on the other end. "Hello?"

"Hi...uh, this is Madge."

"Yeah, it is Karyn. How are you?"

"Honestly, I have been better. But I am calling because Granny came to visit me the other day, and she said that Nichole had a hearing yesterday. What happened?"

Karyn looked over at Nichole sitting on the floor beside the table, petting Zamu. "It went well. She is here now."

"Really? Oh, thank God! I cannot lose my baby, Karyn. I am so ready to change and be the mother she deserves."

"Yeah, she is pretty great, and she needs you. But we are going to take care of her until you are ready. And you will need to really be ready, okay?"

"Yes, yes. I am going to stay away from Andy when I get out, and I am going to get a job and a place to live and whatever it takes."

"I am glad to hear that. The court is ordering monitored visits at first."

"I can do that." Madge agreed. "Can I talk to her now, though? I do not want her to see me here, but if I can just talk to her this once."

"Okay," Karyn pulled the phone away from her ear. "Nichole, it is for you. It is your mom."

Nichole sprang to her feet, grabbed the phone, and pressed it to her ear. "Mommy?"

"Yes, Baby. It's me. How are you?"

"I am doing okay. I get to live with Granny and Grandpa and Aunt Karyn for a while."

"That is good, Baby. I am so glad to hear your voice."

"Guess what, Mommy! They saved Chloe! She lives here too now."

"Wow! Did they really do that? That is so great." Madge's voice cracked as she tried to conceal that she was crying on the other end of the phone.

"Yeah, are you okay, Mommy?"

"Yeah, Baby. I am doing real good. And I am going to keep doing good. After I get out of here, we will be together again. Okay?"

"Yeah, okay."

"Good. But for now, I need you to be good for your grandparents and your aunt. They will give you a really good home."

"I know, Mommy. You need to get better so that we can be a family again."

"And I will. I promise you that."

"I love you, Mommy."

"I love you more, Baby."

"I love you the mostest, Mommy."

Madge laughed. "Okay, I have to go now. Be good."

"I will. Bye, Mommy."

Nichole handed the phone back to her aunt and sat back on the floor with the dog.

Karyn hung up the phone on the receiver and sat down next to Nichole. "Are you okay, Sweetie?"

"Yeah," Nichole looked at her. "My mommy is getting better, and I have a new home. Everything is wonderful."

Nichole crawled from where she sat on the floor, climbed onto her aunt's lap, and hugged her. She stroked Nichole's head. "Yes, you are home. And your mom is going to get better soon."

Made in the USA
Lexington, KY
31 July 2016